ANCHORS
FOR THE
Soul

"If you are looking for a guide to lead you through your moments of searching for the Holy One, you have found it. Joyce Rupp's beautifully crafted words will companion you: inspiring, inviting, uplifting, and enlightening you day by day. *Anchors for the Soul* proves to be true to its name."

Macrina Wiederkehr
Author of *Seven Sacred Pauses*

"If Joyce Rupp's soulful words over the years have been an anchor and guide for you, this gathering of her wisdom comes as a welcome and bountiful gift. If you are new to her writing, this is a wonderful entry point to have her companion you through all the days of the year. I highly recommend this rich volume to anyone longing for grace and insight to bless their days."

Christine Valters Paintner
Author of *The Artist's Rule*

"Drawing upon wisdom from some of her most beloved writings, Joyce Rupp offers a feast of daily readings. Filled with the issues she has bravely and beautifully explored, her writings are the fruit of her exceptional journey and an invitation to discover peace in our own centers."

Paula D'Arcy
Author of *Winter of the Heart*

"This important resource collects so much of Joyce Rupp's wisdom in such a usable day-by-day format. As someone who has read almost all of Rupp's work, I'm grateful that compiler Kathy Reardon has selected the best of the best for these daily reflections. Whether used as spiritual reading first thing in the morning, as a prayer companion before bed, or for a quick check-in during the day, these spiritual snippets can really help people stay anchored and grounded, especially in these tumultuous times."

Heidi Schlumpf
Columnist with the *National Catholic Reporter*

ANCHORS
FOR THE
Soul

DAILY WISDOM

FOR INSPIRATION

AND GUIDANCE

JOYCE RUPP
Compiled by Kathy Reardon

SORIN BOOKS  Notre Dame, IN

---

www.sorinbooks.com

Paperback: ISBN-13 978-1-932057-12-6

E-book: ISBN-13 978-1-932057-13-3

Cover image © Getty Images.

Cover and text design by Brian C. Conley.

Printed and bound in the United States of America.

Library of Congress Cataloging-in-Publication Data
Names: Rupp, Joyce, author. | Reardon, Kathy, author.
Title: Anchors for the soul : daily wisdom for inspiration and guidance / Joyce Rupp ; compiled by Kathy Reardon.
Description: Sorin Books Notre Dame, IN : Sorin Books, [2018] | Includes index.
Identifiers: LCCN 2018014335 (print) | LCCN 2018021970 (ebook) | ISBN 9781932057126 | ISBN 9781932057126 (paperback) | ISBN 9781932057133 (ebook)
Subjects: LCSH: Devotional calendars.
Classification: LCC BV4811 (ebook) | LCC BV4811 .R759 2018 (print) | DDC 242/.2--dc23
LC record available at https://lccn.loc.gov/2018014335

CONTENTS

Preface

*A spiritual life is simply a life in which all that
we do comes from the center, where we are all
anchored in God.*

—Evelyn Underhill

*Is there a quiet stream underneath the fluctu-
ating affirmations and rejections of my little
world? Is there a still point where my life is
anchored and from which I can reach out with
hope and courage and confidence?*

—Henri J. M. Nouwen

More than twenty years ago, I flew to San Diego, Califor-
nia, to make an eight-day silent retreat. During that spiritually fruitful period, I often sought quiet time by going
to sit on a large rock by the beach. No matter what time of
day I went there, a small sailboat sat anchored in the same
place. It was tethered quite a distance from the shore and
rested in my direct line of vision. I can vividly call forth
that image in my memory because of what I experienced
as I observed the boat's presence every day. In high or
low tide it remained right where it was. If the waves were
calm, little movement occurred. When the ocean experienced wild winds or stormy weather, the sailboat might
bounce around a lot, but it stayed securely moored. Nothing pushed the craft out to sea because of how strongly it
was anchored.

By the end of the retreat the anchored sailboat had
become a symbol of my desire to stay firmly united with

the Holy One. I knew without a doubt that when I departed and returned home my life would not always contain tranquility. Like the many moods of an ocean, there would sometimes be stormy, blustery weather to toss my thoughts and emotions around when things did not go well. I asked myself, "How will I maintain peacefulness and stay confident interiorly when events are turning my world upside down?"

Before leaving San Diego, I made a resolution to be faithful to morning meditation and spiritual reading, no matter what else might be taking place later in the day. This decision has kept my inner boat steady in the fluctuating waters of life. After prayer time, I almost always leave with inspiration and encouragement as I go toward the work that awaits me, having once more been anchored in the love of Ageless Serenity.

Our society today does not make it easy to stay consciously united to the Holy One. So much distracts our minds and hearts from being fixed on what is truly of value. Countless political, social, religious, and cultural tempests try to rip us from our spiritual moorings. My hope in offering *Anchors for the Soul* is that you will reserve some time each day to re-anchor yourself interiorly and that you may find inspiration and insight to steady your spiritual sailboat.

The selections that Kathy Reardon gathered in *Anchors for the Soul* come from a variety of my publications. Some of the readings you will find more helpful than others. Each one is offered as an anchor to tether you to the Holy One. Stay with a selection for as long as you wish, even though it is assigned to a particular day. Skip those that do not appeal to you. Return to what assists you in remaining centered when the turbulent waters of your realm threaten to pull you away from the Source of Peace. I hope that what you find here will enable you to sustain the still point within yourself, as Henri Nouwen suggests, and that you will then "reach out with hope and courage and confidence" to a world much in need of your anchored peacefulness.

—Joyce Rupp

JANUARY 1

The New Year

Guardian of this new year,
I set aside my fears, worries, concerns.
I open my life to mystery, to beauty,
to hospitality, to questions,
to the endless opportunity
of discovering you in my relationships,
and to all the silent wisps of wonder
that will draw me to your heart.

Today: I move beyond concerns and worries.

Out of the Ordinary, p. 145

Being on the Road

Our life is a journey.
We are always on the road.
Each time another January greets us,
we have an opportunity to pause,
to see where we have been,
to notice how far we have come
and ponder how that journey has been for us.

Today: I reflect on how my journey has been.

May I Have This Dance?, p. 20

JANUARY 3

At the Gate of the New Year

Sacred Mystery,
waiting on the threshold
of this new year,
you open the gates
and beckon to me:

"Come! Come!
Be not wary of what awaits you
as you enter the unknown terrain;
be not doubtful of your ability
to grow from its joys and sorrows.
For I am with you.
I will be your Guide.
I will be your Protector.
You will never be alone."

Today: I remember that I am never alone.

Out of the Ordinary, p. 145

January 4

Freshness

If we are to walk into the new year with hope,
we need to look to God, as well as ourselves.
When we look to the scriptures we learn
how much God desires new beginnings for us.
This is a constant theme through the sacred Word.
God refreshes, renews, heals, blesses, makes whole,
cleanses what has become mired,
clears what has become blurred,
restores what has died,
recovers what has gone astray.

Today: I renew my relationship with the Holy One.

Fresh Bread, p. 20

JANUARY 5

Looking Back

As you look back on the year just completed:

What name would you give to last year's journey?
How would you describe it to one of your friends?
What image or metaphor would you use to talk about it?
Who were your wise persons?
What did they reveal to you?
How did this influence your life?

What was most satisfying about the year?
What was least satisfying?

Today: I look at my past year and learn from it.

Out of the Ordinary, p. 146

Guiding Star

Like the wise ones who sought the Christ Child,
I have trekked for eons in the aimless dark,
Moving by faith within my inner landscapes,
Without a detailed map and full of questions.
In spite of all that seems void and doubtful,
My seeking of you has never been halted.
When the searching path to you grows faint,
You appear as my trusted Guiding Star.
A beacon of hope beckoning me onward
Manifesting your presence in surprising ways.

Today: I follow my inner Guiding Star.

Fragments of Your Ancient Name, January 8

Trust in the Journey

As we enter the new year,
we trust God with our lives.
We trust that there will be
enough strength and beauty
amid all the pain
to sustain us
and to urge us forward.
We trust that we will come
to greater wholeness
and transformation.

Today: I notice what keeps me from trusting.

May I Have This Dance?, p. 26

JANUARY 8

Looking Forward

As you look to the year before you:

How do you want to name your new year?
What gifts do you bring with you?
Of what are you most afraid as you enter this year?
What is your greatest need for the coming year?
Who do you bring with you for your support?
What is at the heart of your new year's prayer?

Today: I enter into my hopes for the new year.

Out of the Ordinary, p. 146

JANUARY 9

A Clearer Vision

Each new year is the time to clear our vision,
to take stock of our resources
and refresh our dreams
as we set out once more on the journey
that is ours.

We may feel stuck in a rut, facing a dead end,
or caught up in a very ordinary pattern of life.
Yet, if we pause to look deeper,
to examine our life more closely,
we will see that many people and events
called us to growth.

Today: I pray for clear vision in the new year.

May I Have This Dance?, p. 20

Prayer of the New Year

Faithful Companion, in this new year I pray:

to live deeply, with purpose,
to live freely, with detachment,
to live wisely, with humility,
to live justly, with compassion,
to live lovingly, with fidelity,
to live mindfully, with awareness,
to live gratefully, with generosity,
to live fully, with enthusiasm.

Today: I renew my intention to live these virtues.

Out of the Ordinary, p. 144

Enter the Unknown

Whenever we walk into a new year,
we are invited to enter into the unknown.
We do not know what events
will surprise us along the way.
We can only see life for today.
But we can risk the road
because we have tremendous assurance
that God goes with us on the journey.

"Be confident. For go where you will,
your God is with you" (Jos 1:9).

Today: I pray to be open to the new year's surprises.

May I Have This Dance?, p. 26

The Quiet Spaces

The quiet spaces in my life
are necessary
if there is to be movement
from the head to the heart,
for it is in the heart
that wisdoms are born.
I can know and experience many things,
but they remain only knowledge
until I allow them
to sink into the depths of my heart,
there to toss and to turn,
to weep and to wail,
to leap and to dance.

Today: I take time for quiet reflection.

The Star in My Heart, p. xxiv

JANUARY 13

Pinnacles of Winter

Pinnacles of translucent winter
hang from the cottage roof,
fierce as untouchable swords,
strong enough to slice off a hand,
daring anyone to cling
for more than a momentary touch.

They patter steadily on the wet ledge,
their strength melting in the January sunshine,
surrendering themselves to annihilation
like a weathered crone sighing love songs
on her death bed.

Today: My sharp edges melt a bit.

My Soul Feels Lean, p. 47

JANUARY 14

Spirit of Freedom
inside each of us
there awaits a wonder
full
spirit of freedom

she waits
to dance
in the rooms
of our heart
that are closed,
dark and cluttered

Today: I empty a bit more of the clutter from my heart.

The Star in My Heart, p. 76

JANUARY 15

Wonderfully Made

Dear God,
you created me as a human person
whose journey of life is the path to wholeness.
This journey needs room for growth
and space for evolving discovery.
Each day is another opportunity
to receive your help and your love,
as I become the person I am meant to be.
Help me to love myself well
and to entrust my growth to your guidance.

Today: I remember that I am "wonderfully made" (Ps 139:14).

The Cup of Our Life, p. 57

Releasing Old Burdens

Faithful Guide,
As I attend to the old burdens
that have weighed me down with worry,
I look ahead with hopeful expectation
to what my heart most needs.
I also recognize the absolute necessity
of living in the present moment.
I choose to direct my daily attentiveness
toward what will give my life greater balance.
I seek to let go of what keeps me unloving.
I long to contribute to peace in this world.

Today: I will release a burden that weighs me down.

Prayers to Sophia, p. 12

January 17

Energizing Wisdom

Sophia, holy Wisdom,
a life-giving energy in my spirit,
coaxes, urges, encourages me
to come into the deep recesses
where I have not yet been transformed.

She guides me inward, saying,
"Do not fear: be of great courage;
you will find blessings for your spirit
in these dark places of your deepest self.
You will bring them up into the light
and discover they are your greatest treasures."

Today: I pay attention to what is being coaxed forth.

The Star in My Heart, pp. xxiv–xxv

A Robin in January

I pause, look again.
Yes, a robin in January,
out of place, out of time,
perched on a low branch,
feathers fluffed, looking calm.

A robin in winter seems
no harbinger of spring,
no sign of hope.
Rather, a witness to courage
or missed opportunity.

Either way, I stand amazed
and wonder what that robin
has to say to my own journey.

Today: I name my mentors of courage.

My Soul Feels Lean, p. 141

JANUARY 19

Reclaiming Wholeness

Wholeness implies a process,
a gradual coming together into a oneness
in which all the parts are integrated,
but not necessarily perfect.
Wholeness or holiness takes a lifetime
of ups and downs.
It can never be accomplished
apart from divine help and guidance
or without the interaction of our lives
with others.

Today: I am at home with myself.

The Cup of Our Life, p. 55

Celebrate Wonder

Creator of wintry ice and snow,
The untamed winds of frosted winter
Cough their way into penetrating coldness.
Heavy snowflakes swirl wildly everywhere.
You invite us to witness this fresh beauty,
To lessen complaint about its inconvenience.
You speak to grumbling hearts in this season:
"Celebrate the wonder of what is before you.
Abandon your schedules and organized plans.
Settle into the long wintry evenings of quiet
And sip the good red wine of my contentment."

Today: I find a place of contentment within myself.

Fragments of Your Ancient Name, January 19

Comfort on Dreary Days

Eternal Presence,
you are with me on my journey.
You know the loneliness
that wraps around my heart
and leaves a void of sadness.
Comfort me on my dreary days
when emptiness is all I know.
Do not let me succumb
to isolated self-pity.
Let me experience your presence.
Fill my downcast spirit with your joy.
Keep me close to your abiding love
with every step I take.

Today: I draw closer to the Eternal Presence.

Your Sorrow Is My Sorrow, p. 173

Simple Things

In the hurry,
in the rush,
simple things missed,
blessings denied,
beauties ignored.

In the calm,
in the quiet,
simple things received,
mystery unfolds,
happiness blooms.

In the peace,
in the harmony,
I taste with love
all that is good.

Today: I receive the goodness of life's simple things.

Rest Your Dreams on a Little Twig, p. 141

Acts of Kindness

Daily acts of kindness, considerate understanding,
and spontaneous generosity may not appear to have
a great effect and yet they have the power to ease
the pain of negativity and cradle a buoyancy in
another person's heart.

We never know what one thoughtful act of kindness
might engender in the life of another,
or how far-reaching that deed might be.

Today: I intentionally extend a kindness to someone.

Boundless Compassion, p. 161

What Will I Choose?

Adventure depends on openness
and an attitude of risk taking.
Life can be boring and yawningly predictable
or it can be surprisingly eventful
and growth-filled.
It depends on how we see it
and what we allow it to be for us.
The landscape of our daily routines
may be the same
but we are never the same inside.
There is always something new waiting for us,
if we will open ourselves to it.

Today: A spirit of adventure awakens in me.

Walk in a Relaxed Manner, p. 78

January 25

Ongoing Transformation

There on the boulders I pondered life and death.
I reviewed who I had become and wondered
how I wanted to live out the rest of my days.
All those lessons along the way
were too powerful to set aside.
So were the difficulties I encountered.
I felt badly about my response to the struggles.
I wished I had been more of a "model" pilgrim.
My impatience and my inability to accept
the unwanted aspects of the Camino
told me of my unfinishedness
and need for ongoing transformation.
I said to myself,
"I'd better 'get with it' before I die."

Today: I look at what part of my life needs to "get with it."

Walk in a Relaxed Manner, p. 254

The Path of Love

Each day the Dawn-Bringer calls to us:
"Open the door. Explore what you believe and know.
Investigate what you do not believe and do not know.
Seek my dawning light within the fragments
of your daily happenings.
Search within yourself for paths that lead to love.
Lift the shades off the windows
of your shadowy heart-room.
Welcome the coming of each secret
that shows its face to you.
Venture into illuminating self-acceptance
so more of my radiant beauty shines forth from you."

Today: I take a path that leads to love.

Open the Door, p. 80

Where Is My Enthusiasm?

As I review the year,
I look for what allows my life
to receive greater meaning
and what resists it.
I wander through the months recalling
who and what gave me strength
and where enthusiasm ripened
or died on the vine.

I look for graced moments
that I have totally forgotten,
those spaces in my days
when I am swept off my controlled feet
by the grace of a tender God who says,
"Don't forget you are in my heart."

Today: I take a look at my enthusiasm.

Out of the Ordinary, p. 143

Memories of Winter

The winters of my childhood that I remember most vividly
are the years before we had indoor plumbing and television.
I do not recall feeling deprived during those years.
Winter was simply a part of life, one of the four seasons,
and it seemed natural to adapt to the way
that winter expressed itself.

In the deepest part of winter, the sun set in late afternoon
and the stars would be strong in the clear blue sky.
The stars easily spoke to me, something wordless
I could never have named,
but powerful and comforting at the same time.
It was like old friends greeting and blessing me
as I walked from the barn to the house.

Today: I welcome winter's beauty.

The Circle of Life, pp. 237–238

January 29

Listening Deeply

Winter, humble servant of creation,
you call us to sit by the fireplace
and feed each other stories.

You invite us to listen
to that which is invisible.

You are the contemplative season.
Share with us your virtues
of solitude, contemplation, and faith.

Today: I am intent on listening more deeply.

The Circle of Life, pp. 25-26

The Gift of a Threshold

The metaphor of the threshold aptly describes
a vital component of our spiritual journey.
The gift of the threshold provides a way
to cross over into a fuller life
of spiritual depth and freedom.
When we choose to traverse the invisible boundary
of the known self and enter the unknown,
we are saying: Yes, I want to grow, to become wiser,
to be strengthened, to be less burdened
by what weighs me down
and keeps me from being my authentic self.
I am willing to pay the price for this growth.

Today: I renew my desire to continue to grow spiritually.

Open the Door, pp. 92, 94

JANUARY 31

A Prayer for Openness

Open my mind
to remember your presence.

Open my mouth
to speak your wisdom.

Open my heart
to extend your love.

Open my hands
to serve you generously.

Open my whole being to you.

Today: I am open to the Holy One's presence.

Open the Door, p. 13

Beckoner

You tap at the window of my heart.
You knock at the door of my busyness.
You call out in my night dreams.
You whisper in my haphazard prayer.
You beckon. You invite. You entice.
You woo. You holler. You insist:
"Come! Come into my waiting embrace.
Rest your turmoil in my easy silence.
Put aside your heavy bag of burdens.
Accept the simple peace I offer you."

Today: I respond to the One who beckons me.

Fragments of Your Ancient Name, February 1

FEBRUARY 2

Peaceful Presence

When inner turmoil and conflict
threaten my peace of mind and heart,

When I enter into the pain and the suffering
of the world's lack of peace,

When I hurt for friends, relatives, and others
who are distressed,

When fear of the future rises up
and the way ahead is uncertain and unsettled,

When I feel a distance from the One
who is the fullness of peace,

May your peace grow ever stronger in me.

Today: I rest in the Peace-Giver's presence.

Prayer Seeds, p. 60

February 3

Solitude

Solitude is the empty space we deliberately choose
in order to be with the Beloved.
Here we can savor this goodness
and give ourselves space to really listen.
When we are occupied with life's many details
and rushing about in the marketplace,
only the surface things usually get our attention.
Solitude can help us to disengage and detach.
It is when we are alone,
uninterrupted, single-minded and single-hearted,
that some wonderful inner fruits come to the surface.

Today: I choose some time to be in solitude.

The Cup of Our Life, p. 47

Psalm for a Winter Day

Creator of all seasons and ages,
I praise you for all that is beautiful
in this winter day of February coldness:
the strong, black patterns of trees standing tall,
utter whiteness of snow as it layers the lawn,
stillness broken only by the sound of the furnace
and maybe a brave cheep of the snowbird,
blue sky with morning pink still on its cheek,
the bush under the rainspout drenched in ice.

All the winter world, whose beauty we so often miss,
whose weather we so often condemn,
praise the Creator,
for our world has wonders and tiny miracles
if only our hearts and eyes are open to see.

Today: My heart rejoices in the beauty of creation.

Fresh Bread, p. 38

FEBRUARY 5

I Arise

I arise today with gratitude for life.
I arise with hope that all shall be well.
I arise with courage to meet what will be difficult.
I arise with conviction to do what is life-giving.
I arise with eyes ever alert for beauty.
I arise with openness to greater truth.
I arise with desire for continued transformation.
I arise with compassion for hurting ones.
I arise with willingness to help those who need my care.
I arise with love for the Holy One, my Intimate Companion.

Today: Love spills forth from my heart.

Out of the Ordinary, p. 142

FEBRUARY 6

Darkness That Instills Growth

Darkness exists as a natural part of life,
but I fought this reality for years.
It always seemed like a powerful intruder
into my light-filled life.
I had this notion that if I thought
or did the right things,
then my life would always unfold
the way I wished;
I could avoid anguishing, bleak times.
Consequently, when the dark moments showed up,
I felt something must be terribly wrong with me.
I presumed I had failed in some significant way
because I had not figured out
how to keep darkness from invading my life.
It has taken a long time for me to acknowledge
darkness as an essential element for personal growth.

Today: I consider how dark times helped me to grow.

Little Pieces of Light, p. 2

Sentinel of Hope

Evergreen
silent sentinel of hope
through all seasons.

Somewhere
deep within me
an evergreen grows,
strong, tall, resilient,
always singing
of life.

Her stouthearted green
endures, thrives
amid winter wilds.

She is strong.
She is evergreen.
She lives in me.

Today: A silent sentinel of hope lives in me.

Rest Your Dreams on a Little Twig, p. 33

FEBRUARY 8

Letting Go of Grumbling

"You have only to keep still" (Ex 14:14).

This is no easy thing when we are struggling
to be in control and life keeps getting messier
and more out of control.
What happens if we stop grumbling
and attacking our difficult circumstances?
What happens when we are "still,"
when we turn to the One who promises to care for us?
Our situation will not change instantly,
but we will have greater peace of mind
and more love in our hearts.

Today: I let go of what I cannot control.

Inviting God In, p. 151

The Journey to the Heart

I asked God if I could do it,
if I could really go deeper.
It seemed that God said: "If you want to, you can."
It was then that I stood on the hillside in the desert
and praised God who had visited me,
who had revealed the call
to go more deeply into the divine heart
by going more deeply into my own.

Today: I move more deeply into my heart.

Dear Heart, Come Home, p. 26

Winter's Cloak

This year I do not want
the dark to leave me.
I need its wrap
of silent stillness,
its cloak
of long-lasting embrace.
Too much light
has pulled me away
from the chamber
of gestation.

Today: I wrap winter's cloak around me.

The Circle of Life, p. 249

The Cave of the Soul

Let the dawns
come late,
let the sunsets
arrive early,
let the evenings
extend themselves
while I lean
into the abyss of my being.

Let me lie in the cave
of my soul,
for too much light
blinds me,
steals the source
of revelation.

Let me seek solace
in the empty places
of winter's passage,
those vast dark nights
that never fail to shelter me.

Today: I welcome the grace of winter's solace.

The Circle of Life, pp. 249-250

February 12

Radiant Love

When we open the door of our heart
to what beckons us inward,
we become adventurers
of the unknown territory of our being.

The more we enter our core reality,
the more the true self
becomes available to us.

All the opened places of the heart
eventually move us
into oneness with radiant Love.

Today: I unite with radiant Love.

Open the Door, p. 79

Choosing Freely

One of the best things about inner freedom
is the ability to be less controlled by our emotions
or our ideas, to be able to sort them out
and to see what leads to greater good.
It is the gift of deliberately choosing
to act in a certain way,
not out of guilt, fear, coercion, manipulation,
or any other unfree motivation,
but because we *want* to do so.
When we have inner freedom, we are able
to dwell more quietly at our center
because we are more true to who we really are.

Today: I recognize my power to choose freely.

The Star in My Heart, p. 84

FEBRUARY 14

Becoming

To be free inside is to know and accept
the person we are becoming.
It is to have a vision of life and self
that moves us toward goodness and wholeness,
always drawing us into bonding
with all that is good in the world.
When our true self is freed,
we are a blessing to others,
often without realizing it,
because the peace at our center
comes through to the other.

Today: My heart's desire is to be a blessing to others.

The Star in My Heart, pp. 84–85

FEBRUARY 15

Trusted Guide

If only I would keep in mind
That you are there beside me
When I am searching for a way,
Struggling with a decision,
Wondering about a response.
If only I would trust you
To inform my decisions,
To influence my insights,
To guard my heart's direction.
If only I would trust you.

Today: I renew trust in my Inner Guide.

Fragments of Your Ancient Name, August 5

Opening the Inner Door

When we open the door of our heart
to what beckons us inward, we become adventurers
of the unknown territory of our being.
We do not stay with what is identified and secure.
Like the dawn bringing illumination to the day,
the journey to our authentic self
holds countless findings waiting to enlighten us.
The doors we open ultimately lead
to the genuine nucleus of our self,
affording us the opportunity
to shed the falseness to which we once tightly clung.

Today: I travel beyond the boundaries of my known self.

Open the Door, p. 79

February 17

Frozen Songs

the music of the winter birds
waits in silent throats,
frozen in quiet crystals
of falling snow.

few warbles or chattering chirps
greet the shivering sunrise,
no luring of demure mates
as in the warm frenzy of spring.

like the birds, my silenced soul
stores her muffled songs,
resting them in the dark solitude
of icy vigil,

waiting, as we all do,
for the softening of heart
and the greening
of what has long been lost
to hibernated joy.

Today: I turn gently toward my hibernated joy.

My Soul Feels Lean, p. 110

FEBRUARY 18

A Nudge to Grow

Any kind of darkness can call, push, nudge,
and urge us onto the path of inner growth.
It wakes us up and stirs questions in us
we would rather not face.

How do the patterns of my thoughts
and behaviors influence my life?

Whom or what have I hurt or taken for granted?

Have I been attentive to the deepest longings
of my soul?

What asks to be let go in order for me to find peace?

How is fear influencing my response?

What do I really want to do with my life?

Today: I reflect on one of these questions.

Little Pieces of Light, pp. 11-12

Leaning on the Heart of God

I am leaning on the heart of God.
I am resting there in silence.
All the turmoil that exhausts me
is brought to bear on this great love.

No resistance or complaint is heard
as I lean upon God's welcome.
There is gladness for my coming.
There is comfort for my pain.

No miracle of instant recovery.
No taking away of life's burdens.
Yet, there is solace for my soul,
and refuge for my exiled tears.

Today: I lean on the compassionate heart of God.

Out of the Ordinary, p. 61

Breath of Life

God is as near to us as every breath we take.

Our breath constantly provides a reminder
of our communion with God.
The pattern of our breathing
presents an attentive focus in prayer,
keeping us mindful of the One who dwells with us.

Breath of Life,
you ride the waves of life with me
in the rhythms of my communion with you.
You enter the comings and goings
of each day and in every prayer I breathe.
Whether I am in the stillness of quiet prayer
or in the fullness of the day's activity,
may your peace flow through my being.

Today: My breath leads me to attentive prayer.

Prayer, pp. 60, 62

The Search

I search for vision
in the shadows of my soul,
impatiently awaiting
the moment of lighting.

I search for a quiet heart
amid life's harried schedule;
my soul cries out,
yearning for solitude.

I search for compassion
in a world gone deaf
to the cries of the hurting,
and the pleas of the powerless.

I search for Home,
always for Home,
unaware, of course,
that I am already there.

Today: I recognize what I have already found.

May I Have This Dance?, pp. 92-93

Changing the Landscape

It doesn't take much
to change the gray drabness
of a bleak winter day,

just an inch or two of snow
upon the lawn and roof.

It doesn't take much
to change the stony landscape
of a rankled heart,

just a word or two of kindness
soft upon the discontent.

Today: I offer kindness where I can.

My Soul Feels Lean, p. 116

February 23

A Cosmic Blessing

Through the ages people have been drawn
to the lights of the heavens,
not only because these lights
comfort and guide in darkness,
but because these vast twinkling masses of light
evoke a cosmic mystery.
They stand as messengers
of some limitless connection beyond human perception.

As I stand in my own small space of the planet,
reveling in the power and beauty of the heavens,
I feel a great unity with all beings.

Today: The beauty of the cosmos fills me with awe.

The Cosmic Dance, pp. 44–46

Season of Waiting

Winter is the season of waiting.
It requires great trust and a willingness
to believe that this angst will not last forever.
Even though all appears dead and void of movement,
there is quiet growth taking place.

During the darkness, gestation occurs.
In the caves and hidden hollows of winter,
baby bears are born. In the frozen air,
branches with terminal buds secretly grow every day.
In the unmoving soil, flower bulbs are strengthened
for their future journey upward toward the sun.
In the frozen human heart, silent seeds of confidence
are prepared for amazing new growth.

Today: I trust the gestation of my spiritual growth.

The Circle of Life, p. 230

FEBRUARY 25

Jewels of Wisdom

The inner world contains landscapes
of clarity and rivers of knowledge,
shadowed caves with unwanted
and unclaimed characteristics
waiting to teach us, jewels of wisdom
containing strength and guidance,
an air of enticement that forever lures us
toward union with the Divine Muse.

We spend most of our waking life
with a focus on our external world.
How much richer our life would be
if we gave equal time to the internal reality.

Today: I believe I have inner treasures of wisdom.

Open the Door, p. 18

Being Nonjudgmental

We all need to make choices and decisions
that affect our lives. However, when we compare
our values, beliefs, and opinions to how others
ought to look, speak, and act—and become critical
when they do not meet our criteria—
judgment becomes divisive and noncompassionate.
How quickly we can get caught in comparing
and categorizing others according to our biases.
This negative valuing adds to, rather than lessens,
individual and global suffering. Harsh judgment
keeps love at a distance and blocks peace.

Today: I am careful about the judgments I make.

Boundless Compassion, p. 23

FEBRUARY 27

Facets of Prayer

Many years pass before we really believe
our connectedness to the Holy One
is enduring and true.
Even when we do believe this,
cloudy times of questioning the worth
and effectiveness of our relationship with God
are not unusual.

On the other hand, sometimes our prayer life
offers us profound consolation in which
we become convinced that this relationship
is solid and enduring.

"Prayer" is not only about entering
into a relationship with God;
it is also about *being changed*.
Healthy prayer strengthens our bond
with the Creator
and it also transforms us.

Today: I desire to grow in relationship with God.

Prayer, pp. 19-20

February 28

Seeking Balance

Joy, beauty, happiness, gratitude, understanding,
and a sense of purpose and meaning—
these await our reception if we turn in their direction.
We lose hope if our only focus is on suffering.
To retain energy and strength
in expressing compassion day by day,
we must have balance.

We must be intentional about seeking
what soothes our mind and restores our spirit,
while at the same time being ever vigilant
to how we can be compassionate.

Today: I seek for balance throughout the day.

Boundless Compassion, p. 184

FEBRUARY 29

Welcome Home

I entered the sacred inner room
where everything sings of Mystery.
no longer could I deny or resist
the decay of clenching control
and the silent gasps of surrender.

there in that sacred place of my Self
Love of a lasting kind came forth,
embracing me like a long beloved one
come home for the first time.

much that I thought to be "me"
crept to the corners and died.
in its place a Being named Peace
slipped inside and softly spoke my name:
"Welcome home, True Self,
I've been waiting for you."

Today: I welcome home what waits for me.

Dear Heart, Come Home, pp. 9–10

MARCH 1

A Call to Return

I am always amazed at how many people
come to Ash Wednesday services.
Why do they make such an effort to take a lunch hour,
or rise earlier than usual, or come to church
after a day's work when they might not come
to Mass at any other weekday of the year?

Perhaps it is the call to "return."
Maybe a sense of hope is kindled in hearts
by the possibility of coming back to the Holy One
and trying once again to strengthen one's faith.
It may also be the realization
that there is always a part of one's heart
that has not yet been given over to God.

Today: I return to the Friend of my heart.

Inviting God In, p. 46

Draw Me to Your Heart

Occasionally the mystery of God
enters our lives with such surprise and clarity
we have no choice but to move immediately
and totally toward an abiding awareness
of this great love.
For a brief time, we are swept up
in a contemplative movement
that instantly connects our inner and outer worlds.
We cross the threshold where we meet
and merge with divine presence.
It is a sweet, holy, amazing moment.

Today: I long to be drawn toward the heart of God.

Prayer, p. 77

MARCH 3

Anxiety

Calming Sea of Peace,
bits of anxiety rankle my spirit.
They inject distress signals
in all that I attempt to do.
My joy scurries into hiding.
Too much intensity pounds me.
Ego rah-rahs and my soul weeps.
Like the ebbing tide of the ageless sea,
I yearn to be calm, be still,
no fretting or intense beating
against the shore of myself.
Wrap your care around my worries.

Today: I surrender any anxiety to the Peaceful One.

Prayers to Sophia, pp. 14–15

Shepherd

I have been in that bleak valley
When the last bit of joyfulness
Was sucked out of my spirit
By the ripping winds of desolation.
In those times of extended anguish
The memory of green pastures
With you shepherding my way
Brought me strength to go on.
Shepherd, now, others in need
As they stumble on their dark road.

Today: I pray for those who need shepherding.

Fragments of Your Ancient Name, April 4

MARCH 5

The Consolers

Comforting and consoling God,
thank you for those people
who ease the burdens
of difficult times in our lives.
Thank you for those who understand
the pain and the struggles.
Thank you for each one
who has been patient and kind,
for each one who has tried to ease the hurt
and to be there for us.
Thank you for being with us
in your many human disguises.

Today: I am grateful for those who ease burdens.

May I Walk You Home?, p. 121

Listening for Divine Wisdom

It is easy to deceive ourselves
as we walk on our spiritual path.
Because we are flawed human creatures,
we can get sidetracked.
We lose our focus and get caught
in huge self-improvement programs
of our own making
that have little to do with God's desires for us.
Divine guidance is a source of wisdom
that helps us know when to embrace ourselves
and when to not give in to ourselves.

Today: I listen to the inner voice of divine wisdom.

The Cup of Our Life, p. 86

Lost Treasure

Dear Holy One,
please find for me the things I've lost.
Find for me a heart of hope and of trust.

Find a love that runs silent and strong
through dark days as well as bright.
Find a ribbon of truth to tie around
each fragment of my life.
Find a joy and a peace that I can give
to every hurting person.

And please find for me a faith
that is big enough, mellow enough,
to admit my wrongs and to trust
that you will find and welcome me home.

Today: I trust that what is lost in myself will be found.

Fresh Bread, p. 50

A God Who Cares

When we experience our goodbyes,
we come face-to-face with questions
about suffering.
We also come face-to-face with a God
who suffers pain and hurts with us,
a God who wants us to be free of our suffering.

Jesus gave evidence of this in his life
by blessing and healing, freeing and consoling,
doing all he could to take away the suffering
that was part of the human condition.

God is a refuge for the needy in distress,
a shelter from the storm, a shade from the heat,
the good friend who stays with us
in our struggles and our emptiness.

Today: God is a refuge and shelter for me.

Praying Our Goodbyes, p. 23

Don't Run

Don't run
when faced with
something or someone
that seems like
an adversary

Stay with it
Try to hear it
Let the process unfold
Do not judge
Let it all be

Sooner
or maybe later
what is constricted
will lift its head
and surprise you
with how simple
the truth is

Today: I stay with and learn from what I resist.

My Soul Feels Lean, p. 99

Riding Out Life's Storms

"Lord, save us! We are perishing!" (Mt 8:25).

We all have "violent storms" in our lives
at one time or another.
Sometimes they last only a day,
but sometimes they are excruciatingly long.
What do we do when violent storms come?
How do we respond on a spiritual level?

When the disciples got caught in the storm,
they did not trust the presence of Jesus
would be enough for them. They panicked,
and Jesus chided them for their lack of faith:
Didn't they believe that if he was with them
they would be safe? Did they not know by now
that he would be there for them
in the scary moments of their lives?

Today: I review how faith is evident in my life.

Inviting God In, p. 157

Something Foundational

Little do we know when we are young
what might sustain us as we grow old.
What we either take for granted
or are unaware of in our youth
might well be the very thing
that carries us through
some of the more difficult aspects of life later on.
What is certain is that we will need
something foundational on which to rest
our response to waning energy
and persistent limitation of body, mind, and spirit.
It can keep us grounded
in a positive and peaceful manner.

Today: I am aware of what keeps me grounded.

Fly While You Still Have Wings, p. 87

Rainbow Hope

You dance amid the sky's colorful bow,
Flinging needed hope into the far realms,
A sign to each person in a desperate life
That their pain is not the ultimate end.
Anticipation of the lessening of troubles
Sings through the spectrum of colors
In which you dwell as a bringer of change.
You reside as a bright promise of better days,
Like the parting of dark clouds showing light
After a crushing storm with thrashing rain.

Today: I look for hope in my life.

Fragments of Your Ancient Name, June 18

MARCH 13

Failings and Mistakes

Heart of Mercy,
My mistakes and failings keep me humble.
They chide me with their blaming voices
and pester me with their mocking comments.
They badger me with their poking fingers
of disgrace and condemnation.
They hound me with blame and guilt
and a thousand other recriminations.

Walk with me through my mistakes and failings.
Let me hear your understanding and merciful voice.
We both know I am not a perfect person.
Assure me that I am not a bad person, either.
Keep teaching me about myself, about life, about you,
through these characteristics I would rather not have.
Remind me that they are my friends, not my enemies;
they are my teachers, not my wardens.

Today: I turn to the Heart of Mercy for what is needed.

Prayers to Sophia, p. 36

Carrying Crosses

May I recognize the daily cross that is mine
and carry this burden in a trustful way,
confident that the undesired parts of my life
can be guides to my spiritual growth.
Increase my awareness of false judgments,
the unfair expectations that quickly arise to crowd out
kindness and compassion for myself and others.
Soften any hardness of heart that I have toward another.
Increase my ability to be understanding.
Help me topple walls that prevent forgiveness.
Awaken the undying song of hope in my soul
as I carry my unwanted cross each day
so that even in the worst of times I continue to trust you
to provide what is needed.

Today: I carry my cross, with the Holy One's assistance.

Prayer Seeds, p. 90

Conditions for Discipleship

I have never gotten used to the truth
of discipleship;
that to belong to Jesus means more than
just a good feeling of being cherished and loved.
I still struggle with the fact
that there are conditions for discipleship
and that "following" means some hard demands
and some constant conversion.

To follow Jesus in discipleship
means that we, too, will be people of great love.
We too will lay down our lives for others.
This is the price to be paid for discipleship—
the giving away of our very selves.

Today: I choose to be a person of great love.

Fresh Bread, pp. 117, 119

Let People Come into Your Heart

Jesus praised Nathanael when he met him
because Nathanael had no guile;
he was without deceit.
He was someone on whose heart the message
of Jesus could easily be transcribed and sent.
Jesus praised children, too, for their coming to him.
Children are also transparent and easily
allow others to see their feelings and thoughts.

Like Nathanael, like the children Jesus praised,
we too must be open and allow people to know us
if the characteristics of Jesus are to be seen there.
Let people come into your heart;
help them to meet the One you know and love.
Be a letter from the Christ.

Today: I let people come into my heart.

Fresh Bread, p. 94

MARCH 17

Homecoming

O God of exiles and strangers,
find the homeless parts of me.
Guide them toward yourself
for you are my promised land.

Take the stranger inside of me
and find familiar soil for it.
Keep me mindful of the Emmanuel,
whose sojourn brought me a glimpse of home.

Today: I am attentive to what stirs within me.

May I Have This Dance?, pp. 182–183

Tranquility

All is quiet on the mountain
this late March morning.
Forsythia cry out their colors
while the mist still enfolds them.

Inside of me, it is also quiet.
I feel the aura of stillness
and the beauty of calm waters.
It has been so long since silence
rested her wings in my heart.

The earth has gathered me in her arms,
rocking my weariness to sleep.
Months of running and stumbling
are laid down beside the wooded path;
I lift only the beauty of the present moment,
and when I place it in my heart
all my life looks different to me.

Today: I rest in the silence of my heart.

The Star in My Heart, pp. 12–13

Embrace My Humanness

It is time for me
to see the flaws
of myself
and stop
being alarmed.

It is time for me
to embrace
my humanness,
to love
my incompleteness.

Today: I accept my less-than-perfect self.

The Cup of Our Life, p. 54

MARCH 20

Sustaining Love

Holy One,
your love is strong and enduring.
You would never deliberately harm us,
or bring us grief and heartache.
You desire only good for us.
Like a loving parent, you daily offer us
reassurance, strength, and support.

As we walk this path
filled with challenges and struggles,
your love will sustain us.
You will always be there for us.
You will forever hold us close to your heart.
Thank you for embracing us with your love.

Today: I draw strength from Enduring love.

May I Walk You Home?, pp. 29-30

Finding Stillness

Late March rain
threatens to soon be snow.
All through the dark night
it made its mark on earth.
I look out my window
and the concrete walls
are wet with the falling drops.
They patter away on the rooftop
like an old friend calling home.
I pause to say hello
and feel welcome in my heart.
Come again, I say to the rain,
you gentle me and lift me up,
or is it rather, you send me down,
down to the stillness inside,
down to where I need to be.

Today: I let myself be led into stillness.

Dear Heart, Come Home, p. 27

Discouragement

the demon of discouragement
trips me up in hectic times,
takes my heart apart
and dumps out my hope.

the demon of discouragement
points fingers at my weakness,
jaws his mouth at my errors
and threatens to undo me.

the demon of discouragement
despises rainbows, relishes rancor,
fights to hold my moody darkness
and loves to see me weary.

the demon of discouragement
fails to have the last laugh, though,
for I've too many people of promise
whose loves outlast my struggles.

Today: Discouragement does not have the last word.

Fresh Bread, p. 86

Refusal

She's in the desert, dying
of thirst; you offer her
life-giving water.
She turns away
scornfully.

She's in the wilderness,
starving to death. You offer her
nourishing food,
but she refuses it.

You give up trying
to help.
You do the one thing,
the only thing you can.
You let go
and simply love her.

Today: I focus on loving those I want to change.

My Soul Feels Lean, pp. 20–21

Enough

St. Teresa of Avila prayed that she would
let God be enough for her.
When I have times of emptiness,
I sometimes ask God, "Are you enough for me?
Can I be satisfied with just having you
and not having whomever or whatever
is being emptied out of my life?"

I *do* want God to be enough for me
so that I do not go seeking for things
to take the place of this Loving Presence,
but it is easy to waver and doubt
that "God is enough" in my moments
of insecurity or pain. It's a crazy thing
but as much as I find myself longing for God,
it is sometimes excruciating to have nothing but God.

Today: God is enough for me.

he Cup of Our Life, p. 45

MARCH 25

Dissolving in Tenderness

I have stood before you
On numerous occasions,
Knowing my transgression,
Guilty, fairly convicted.
You reach out mercifully,
Drawing my regret toward you
With a generous reception.
In that moment of pardon,
The falseness in my life
Dissolves in your tenderness.

Today: My transgressions dissolve in divine tenderness.

Fragments of Your Ancient Name, April 11

A Prayer for Strength, Part One

Stronghold of Souls, Unshakable One,
infuse your strength into the places
where I feel the greatest weakness.
Permeate the parts of my life
that continually challenge my patience.
Lessen any tendency in my spirit
that gives way to a loss of hope.
Reinforce awareness of the manifestations
of your presence.
Boost my spirit when I think I cannot manage
what is mine to be and do.

Today: I find my strength in the Unshakable One.

Prayer Seeds, p. 56

MARCH 27

A Prayer for Strength, Part Two

Provider of Purpose, Firm Foundation,
Enduring Love,
support my determination to give the best
of myself to others.
Fortify the forgiveness you have placed
and nurtured in my heart.
Sustain a solid belief that I can get through
what appears to be insurmountable.
Bolster my efforts to be a person
who reaches out to those who suffer.
Foster greater trust in you
when worries and anxieties attempt to prevail.
Impart the courage I need
to change what appears to be unchangeable.

Today: Serene security awaits my reception.

Prayer Seeds, p. 56

Speaking to Mary

Woman of Compassion,
you have been there before me.
You were faced with things you did not understand.
You turned to God in your distress
and pondered your experience in your heart.
I have also encountered the realm of mystery.
I, too, do not understand.
I will also turn and ponder this in my heart.

Mary, you searched for your beloved child.
You experienced the distress and longing,
the agony of not knowing where he was.
I, too, search and wonder where my treasure is.
I am also longing to find my pearl of great price.
When will I find what I am seeking?

Today: Mary's faith and courage lead me to my own.

Your Sorrow Is My Sorrow, p. 84

MARCH 29

Accepting Imperfection

I now think differently about my flaws.
I see how being fully human is a paradox.
Growing and becoming more of a person
whose life resembles the values of Jesus is essential.
At the same time, my flaws
are some of the greatest treasures,
like grains of sand in shells
that must grate and irritate to become pearls.
My imperfections keep my ego in check.
They remind me daily
of how much I need the grace of God.
They help me to be more understanding
and compassionate with the inadequacies of others.
They also give me the opportunity to continue
to grow and change.
Many times my inadequacies
are what give the real flavor to my life.

Today: I befriend my inadequacies.

The Cup of Our Life, p. 52

March 30

Going through the Wilderness

God of the journey,
we need a burning bush to set our hearts aflame
with deep love of you.
When the road of life seems long and tedious,
when the dying and the rising get to be too much,
be a pillar of fire by night and comforting cloud by day
so that we can not only see the way
but be confident of your gracious presence,
which is our strength and our hope.
Thank you for your nearness to us
and for encouraging us to trust in you.

Today: I trust the Holy One to guide me.

Out of the Ordinary, p. 211

March 31

Images of Shelter

The Hebrew psalms are filled with images of God
as an encircling shield, a shelter,
a stronghold when times are difficult,
a rock, a fortress,
someone who revives our soul
and girds us with strength,
shelters us under an awning
and hides us deep in a protective tent.
God is a comfort in illness
and a light in the darkness.

What a wonderful opportunity we have
to take our struggles to the Holy One
and receive encouragement, strength,
consolation, compassion, understanding,
and full acceptance.

Today: I take my struggles to the Sheltering One.

May I Have This Dance?, p. 56

APRIL 1

Drawing Me Forward

Just as the light has given me morning,
so you, Holy One, have given me hope.
Praise to you for drawing me forward,
encouraging me to bid farewell to the past.

Continue to blow on the embers.
Light the fire again and again.
Flame it bright and full.
Gift me with surrender in love
so that I can be more fully yours.

Today: The Spirit of Renewal ignites my love.

Prayers to Sophia, pp. 48-49

Springtime Prayer

O Dancer of Creation,
the earth awakens to an urgent call to grow.
In the hidden recesses of my wintered spirit,
I, too, hear the humming of your voice,
calling me, wooing my deadness back to life.

My soul yawns, stretches, quickens
as the energy of spring revives my weariness.
I sit with wonder, observing the steady activity,
savoring the colors and shapes of earth's loveliness.
For a while my doubts, anxieties, and worries
become like chapters in some ancient book
whose text no longer claims my full attention.

Today: I let go of doubts, anxieties, and worries.

Prayers to Sophia, pp. 88–89

Mother Hen

Like a mother hen with chicks,
You attentively care for us,
Gathering us under your wing,
Feeding us with wisdom,
Protecting us from harm,
Nursing our wounds,
Teaching us responsibility,
Leading us on the way,
Expecting us to follow,
Trusting us to grow up.

Today: Mother Hen gathers me under her wing.

Fragments of Your Ancient Name, March 20

April 4

Hope

Delight of my Heart,
I grow ever more grateful
as I pause to look over my shoulder
reflecting on days gone by,
seeing how your counsel never leaves me.

Somewhere far down inside,
I feel cherished and welcomed by you.
I believe you are drawing me ever closer,
with the whisper of "Come" in the air.

Today: I am cherished by the Holy One.

Prayers to Sophia, p. 48

Somewhere Within

Somewhere within
the seed has sprouted.
I can feel its movement.
I can sense its energy.

Somewhere within
the rainfall has reached.
My desert is gone.
My dryness has disappeared.

Somewhere within
I have been given life again.
I can say goodbye to emptiness.
I can say hello to fullness.

And so
the circle of my life-journey
has once more
come into its season of spring.

Today: The energy of new life arises in me.

Praying Our Goodbyes, p. 93

Patience

if only I would be
more patient
with the chrysalis
in me,
there could be
beautiful things
coming to life.

I wonder
what keeps me running
from dormancy,
trying to leap
into a butterfly
long before its time,

thus destroying
what could have been
so beautiful.

Today: I wait patiently for my spiritual growth.

Rest Your Dreams on a Little Twig, p. 71

How Did They Know?

How did they know
it was time to push up
through the long-wintered soil?

How did they know
it was the moment to resurrect
while thick layers of stubborn ice
still pressed the bleak ground flat?

But the tulips knew.
They came, rising strongly,
a day after the ice died.

There's a hope-filled place in me
that also knows when to rise.

Today: Like the dormant tulips, hope stirs in me.

The Cosmic Dance, p. 115

APRIL 8

Little Easters

My little Easters are those moments
when something that has died in me
is raised to life again.

It would be easy to pass these things by
or not notice how significant they are to life.
I may not always have a high-in-the-sky feeling
when I celebrate Easter
but I do know they provide quiet reassurances
that God keeps raising dead parts of my spirit to life.

Today: I look for the "little Easters."

Fresh Bread, pp. 57-58

A Hope-Full Prayer

Stream of Love,
all-encompassing,
gathering me
as a cherished one
in a welcoming embrace

Stream of Nurturance,
providing for me
in the darkness
of your protective
enveloping womb

Stream of Joyfulness,
dancing in me
celebrating life
with each moment
of gladness

Today: I enter the Stream of Joyfulness.

Dear Heart, Come Home, p. 155

Put Down the Sword of Busyness

Companion of my Solitude,
sometimes I think that half of me
is well-lodged in another world.
On rainy days, in times of solitude,
my spirit pulls and tugs,
crying for home in that other space.
All the things here
that give my life rhyme and reason
fade from view.
I am left with the longing
to put down my sword
of busyness
and dwell in the land
of simple contemplation.

Today: I am intentional about pausing for quiet time.

Prayers to Sophia, p. 84

Star of Truth

There's a Star inside of me.
She shines there in my heart
and waits to be recognized.

Darkness tries to scare her off,
ego attempts to ignore her,
busyness pushes her around.
But this wonderful shining Star
keeps twinkling, all aglow.

She waits to lead me
to an unknown meadow
where the truth of who I am
will be revealed.

Today: The Star shines brightly within my spirit.

The Star in My Heart, p. 93

APRIL 12

Restoration of Hope

No matter how you are
emotionally, mentally, and physically,
invite hope into your life.
Allow hope to enter into your mind.
Allow hope to enter into your spirit.
Allow hope to enter into your body.
Allow yourself to be filled with hope.

Imagine the Spirit stirring up newness,
finding the dead places that exist within you,
and creating a meadow of flowers there.

Let hope fill your mind with purpose and direction.
Let hope fill your spirit with life and enthusiasm.
Let hope fill your heart and draw you into renewed love.

Today: I rest in a sense of restored hope.

Prayer Seeds, p. 69

APRIL 13

Easter Joy

Joy, come forth in us
like the Risen One
slipping forth
from the darkened tomb.
Come with Easter gladness,
robust power
easily pushing thick stone
from a tight enclosure.

Joy, come dance in us
like the Risen One
showing up unexpectedly.

Today: I welcome the Risen One's joy.

My Soul Feels Lean, p. 119

Resurrection

An unknown Iowa pasture,
two black figures in the dawn,
one large, one very small,
so small as to almost not be seen,
hidden in the fresh folds
of unblemished April grass.

A mother cow gives birth,
leans down, nudges her child,
helps his wobbly legs to stand,
licks away the womb's silk,
and offers the fullness of her udder.

Every day, somewhere,
a new creation.

Today: I awaken to what is birthing in my being.

My Soul Feels Lean, p. 124

Fresh Vitality

Stand in an open doorway, facing east,
the place of the rising sun,
the direction of hope.
Raise your arms.
Move them around in the doorway.
Feel the open space,
the lack of a barrier to your ability
to move freely.

Breathing in, receive the love
of your divine companion.
Accept the fresh vitality
of this enduring presence.
Breathing out, lovingly send this presence
as a gift of hope to all that exists.

Today: I bring hope to each part of my day.

Open the Door, p. 165

Slow Greening

The process of earth's greening
after a long winter
reminds me
of our spiritual "eastering,"
the inner transformation and rebirthing
that comes after we've had
a long winter spell of the spirit.

The dead, brown grass is there for eons
in our hearts, or so it seems.
No amount of hurry, or push, or desire
can make the green happen any sooner.

Each one needs an "eastering,"
a bright greening,
and oh, how they long for it to come soon.

Today: I join with all who long for an "eastering."

Out of the Ordinary, p. 76

Journey of Trust

When we plant a seed in the soil
or when a caterpillar spins a cocoon,
there is no way of telling what's going on inside
or exactly how long the wait is going to be.

We can't dig up the seed to check if there's growth
or slip open the cocoon and peek inside
because each of these actions would cause death.
We can't peer into the tomb of our self
and see if something grows in there either.

It's truly a journey of trust
in the transformative process.
All kinds of inner stirrings go on,
but we simply cannot detect them taking place.

Today: I trust that growth is happening within me.

Little Pieces of Light, p. 31

April Rains

April rains are welcomed
by the thawing winter soil;
almost overnight
the grasses grow green.

They have waited for this moment.

Now everything in them
pushes up and outward
toward the light,
seeking the freedom of growth
like a caged one caught,
finally sprung loose from captivity.

The caged ones within me
are also breaking free.
They are singing spring songs
and dancing in the rain.

Today: I too am greening and breaking free.

Rest Your Dreams on a Little Twig, p. 61

APRIL 19

Reaching to Receive

Personal growth
does take some effort on my part.
I do need to give myself to the process,
but I cannot *force* growth to happen.
This is God's realm of doing.
I can yearn for transformation.
I can be faithful to daily meditation.
But as long as I am trying to go it alone,
I will simply stumble along fruitlessly.

Like the woman who touched the hem
of Jesus' garment and received the healing
power of his spirit, so I need to reach forth
to receive the life-changing energy of divine love.

Today: I touch the hem of Jesus' garment.

The Cup of Our Life, p. 19

A Brief Moment

for a brief moment
early spring rain ceases.
the sun breaks through
gray sky.

threads of gold,
thin enough to pierce
the forest,
glitter on dewdrops,
touching the eyelashes
of blooming forsythia,

making of the yellowed bushes
a place where beauty
bows to brilliance,

where everything arrogant
takes off its shoes
to stand on holy ground.

Today: I stand on holy ground.

My Soul Feels Lean, p. 93

The Door to Growth

Trusted Companion of my journey,
you call me to go through doors of change.
Turn my wavering heart toward you.
Teach me to trust in your guidance.
Convince me of the benefits of change.
Deepen my belief in possibilities of growth.
Most of all strengthen my love for you.
I open the door of my heart to you.
I open the door.

Today: My Trusted Companion strengthens my love.

Open the Door, p. 36

April 22

Our Agenda

In our personal experiences of resurrection,
there resides the element of surrender
and great vulnerability.
We are required to let go of our own agenda.
We would like to plan for the watering
and refreshing of our souls by ourselves.
Just as we find the date for Easter on the calendar,
we want to know when our hearts
will be filled with joy again.

God is with us, providing for us,
watering our inner gardens.
We will not be washed away,
nor will we be left dry forever.
We simply must wait, in hope,
with open minds and hearts.
The rains will come, and when they do,
they will sing in our souls like an Easter alleluia.

Today: I thank God for coaxing me to fuller life.

May I Have This Dance?, pp. 71-72

APRIL 23

The Home of Transformation

Walk past all that hinders kindheartedness
from glowing steadily in my daily routines.
Move into the home of transformation,
into that grace-filled, spacious vessel.
Be restored, repaired, renewed, regenerated.
Come forth with germinating hope, start again
with less control, fewer anticipations,
and more peaceful receptivity
in the container of mind and heart.

Welcome the weak, the hardened, the haughty,
the wounded, the burdened, the pained;
for each and every one of these persons
bears the reflection of my shadowed self,
my own glimpse of what is yet to be purified
in the golden sphere of Christ's love.

Today: I respect each person's spiritual journey.

Prayer Seeds, pp. 95-96

Welcoming New Life

Like a seed trampled underfoot,
You overcame violence and took root.
Like a flower wilted by a freeze,
You lifted your head and newly bloomed.
Like a stream gone dry in drought,
You sought the source and survived.
Like a tree bent over from the storm,
You stood straight and tall again.
Like a faithful lover, returning home,
I welcome your risen presence now.

Today: I welcome the Resurrected One.

Fragments of Your Ancient Name, April 29

Melody of My Soul

At surprising times,
the melody of my buoyant soul
swells to unexpected immensity,
flows through me like April leaves
humming in the breeze.

Merrily the song sways, swings
without a care, in tune
with the mysterious music
sailing through the universe.

This unbounded harmony
tosses my well-calculated life
into tailspins of ecstasy,
lifts me high in happy pursuit
of the singing stars who know
my soul's melody by heart.

Today: I listen to my soul's melody.

My Soul Feels Lean, p. 104

It Is Possible

it is possible
to become so one
with earth
that every flower
perfumes the soul,

every snowflake
sends icy softness
dancing through veins,

every drop of rain
trickles down vessels
of the heart.

it is possible
to become one
with earth.

Today: I enter into oneness with creation.

The Cosmic Dance, p. 20

Awaken Me

Risen One,
come meet me
in the garden of my life.

Raise up neglected gratitude.
Coax my dormant dreams.
Lure me into elation.
Revive my silent hope.
Entice my tired enthusiasm.
Give life to faltering relationships.
Roll back the stone of indifference.
Unwrap deadness in my spiritual life.
Impart heartiness in my work.

Risen One,
send me forth as a disciple
of your unwavering love,
a messenger
of your unlimited joy.

Today: I am a disciple of joy and love.

Out of the Ordinary, p. 70

Fly

Fly, fly
while you still
have wings.

Fly with buoyancy.
Do not falter in fervor
or waver in eagerness.

Lift off with a zestful spirit.

Enter fully what remains
of the fleeting,
diminishing years of life.

Do not wait
to follow what the heart
truly desires.

Today: I desire to have an eager, zestful spirit.

Fly While You Still Have Wings, p. 67

APRIL 29

Seeking Truths

Solitude and reflection are essential
for my inward journey,
but I also need others to help me walk
through the fearsome tunnels of darkness.

In the seasons of my inner life, Sophia's presence
can soften the anguish and isolation of the darkness,
but she will not take it away from me.
The darkness is necessary for my growth.

My fears and anxieties can quietly, or noisily,
tend to take over my decisions and my choices
if there is no awareness of them,
sapping me of my energy for life-giving experiences.

If I stay in the darkness long enough,
my eyes become more accustomed to the dark,
and I begin to see things of beauty and freedom
that I never knew were there.

Today: I recall truths that emerged after difficult times.

The Star in My Heart, p. 8

An Ageless Presence of Peace

Timeless One,
your eternal love wraps courage around us
as we enter into your invitation
to further our spiritual transformation.
Your ageless presence draws us to you
as we step forward,
ready to embrace where you lead us.
Your sustaining peace
rests within our every heartbeat
and accompanies us into the unknown future.
We bow to you with gratitude and confidence.

Today: I cherish the Ageless Presence within me.

Prayer Seeds, pp. 147-148

MAY 1

Selfless Love

Everlasting Love,
within you resides all beneficence.
The generous love I receive from you
inspires and moves me to act unselfishly.
May the goodness dwelling within me
bless the lives of those I daily encounter.
Help me to share my love in spite of the cost.
I open the door of my heart to you.

Today: I focus on acting unselfishly.

Open the Door, pp. 152–153

MAY 2

Holy Mother

Cradle us.
Comfort us.
Nurture us.
Teach us.
Protect us.
Forgive us.
Counsel us.
Celebrate us.
Sustain us.
Love us.

Today: The divine Mother provides for me.

Fragments of Your Ancient Name, May 2

Learning Compassion

Compassionate people
inspire others to be compassionate.

I feel this way
when I meditate on the life of Jesus.
He had an amazing awareness
of people's woundedness.
I marvel at how he was
consistently compassionate
when he met the ill, the grieving,
the hungry, the oppressed.

He is often described
as being "deeply moved in spirit."
The vastness of his ability to love—
and to be loved—is phenomenal.

Today: I am consistently compassionate.

The Cup of Our Life, p. 99

Weather Patterns

I waited long through winter
for the joy of blooming things,
now only to see them crushed
under the weight of unwanted weather.

Perhaps the flowers I seek
must be the deeper ones
that live on in the heart,
where winter snows
do not fall out of season
and harsh raindrops
do not destroy blooming.

But, ah, even there in the heart
the winter weather is unstable.

Today: I accept my inner and outer weather patterns.

Rest Your Dreams on a Little Twig, p. 39

Recognizing Inner Power

Some people lean against fence posts
when their bodies ache from toil.

Some people lean on crutches when
their limbs won't work for them;
and some people lean on each other
when their hearts can't stand alone.

How long it takes to lean upon you,
God of sheltering strength;
how long it takes to recognize the truth
of where my inner power has its source.

Today: I decide to lean, and not to go it alone.

May I Have This Dance?, p. 48

Stillness

stillness

just stillness
like my world seldom knows.
inside I have an expressway
that never slows down,
always full of going somewhere
always another thing to do

stillness

just stillness
filled with quiet, numinous sounds,
like butterfly wings, river murmurs,
cloud breaths, firefly blinks,
and silence, simple, serene silence,
nothing more

Today: I surrender to the call to be still.

The Cosmic Dance, p. 37

Seeing beyond the Familiar

It is easy to seek God in the bliss
of peaceful relationships; in the familiar
comfort of worship, prayers,
the sacraments, and the satisfaction
of successful living.

If I only look for God in the good things of my life,
I will miss many facets of this sacred presence.

I need to focus on the unwanted,
the uncomfortable, and the unexpected
parts of my life to learn that God is there, too.

Today: I look for God in unexpected situations.

Inviting God In, p. 53

Memories

Remembering the goodness of people
has been a source of transformation for me.
When I remember the generosity and kindness
of others, I am deeply touched,
overwhelmed by their ability to be loving,
challenged to be that kind of goodness myself.

During the struggling times, I can so easily forget
the good things that have been part of my life.
Good memories can draw me away
from depression, doubt, and anxiety,
can turn me around to face the joys and blessings
that are there mixed in with the pain.

Today: I spend time with good memories.

The Star in My Heart, pp. 68–69

Through the Dark Woods

The old owl
rests in her home,
waiting for night
to seek nourishment.

Is that what needs
changing
in my life?

I keep expecting
daylight to feed me.
Maybe I, too,
need to fly in the night,
wing through dark woods,
seeking inner nourishment.

Today: I seek opportunities for growth.

Rest Your Dreams on a Little Twig, p. 17

Held in the Arms of the Holy

Picture yourself as a small child
in the arms of the Trustworthy One.
Let yourself be rocked tenderly
in the soft cradle of divine arms.
Hear the Holy One sing a lullaby to you.
Savor this experience.

Today: I am cradled by the Trustworthy One.

Now That You've Gone Home, p. 114

Essence of Love

Evidence is everywhere in my history
that I have been inspired, drawn, carried,
assured, enticed, comforted, nudged.

Now in this stage of our relationship,
you move in the depths of my being,
blend in with the thoughts of my mind,
intermingle in my heart's every beat.

Always you invite me to be true,
to approach life with quiet integrity.

Today: The Essence of Love permeates my being.

Prayer Seeds, p. 173

MAY 12

Generous Gifts

Could I ever truly understand
How much I receive from you?
The fullness of your great love,
The splendor of your creation,
The goodness of your people,
The bounty of your daily grace.
Every day upon my awaking
I receive the bequest of gifts
That I never could have earned,
Given because of your generosity.

Today: I gratefully receive the bequest of gifts.

Fragments of Your Ancient Name, May 31

The Aunts

They came
laden with armfuls
of food
and hearts overflowing
with endless
laughter.

They came
with a sense of well-being
and a generous spirit,
leaving behind
in their own home and heart
tribulations
in need of caring.

They came
not for the purpose
of teaching or preaching,
but to lend a hand
in a troublesome time.

Today: I practice being generous.

Fly While You Still Have Wings, pp. 9–10

Sower of Seeds

May is an excellent time to recognize
more of our potential for wholeness.
It is an excellent time to encourage
that growth in others.

We have the potential to live the values
and virtues of the scriptures.
Our hearts are the soil for these wonderful seeds.
Pray that you can call forth the gifts
of another this springtime.
Pray that you may do so by letting him or her know
the good you see within them.

Today: I look for seeds of goodness in self and others.

Fresh Bread, p. 71

A Prayer for Self-Compassion

The royal law of loving others as ourselves
is quite a challenge.
It requires us to love ourselves well.
I meet many adults who struggle with self-worth.

St. Teresa of Avila developed a prayer
that I find helpful in gaining self-esteem.
Sit in a chair and imagine
Jesus looking upon you with great love.
That's it. Just sit there and be loved.
This is not easy at first, but gradually, day after day,
it becomes less difficult and more acceptable.

As we learn to love ourselves more,
we will find that it is much easier to love others
in a nonjudgmental way, as well.

Today: My Creator looks upon me with devoted love.

Inviting God In, p. 156

Acceptance

When I remember
that God tolerates and forgives
the smelliness of my own faults and failings,
I am more ready to accept
what I find disdainful in others.
The more I know my own great need
for the embrace of a merciful God,
the more I can be forgiving and merciful
to those who wound me.

The more I believe
the Holy One loves and accepts me as I am,
while longing for me to be all I can be,
the more I will gather to my heart
all who are part of this vast world of ours.

Today: I pray to accept those whom I dislike.

Prayer, p. 107

Web of Connection

So much
of this world
lives in
bigger than,
better than,
more than.

Those who are
small
seem to have
no place
among the strong,
the tall,
the sleek.

Yet, each one
has a place,
and all is connected.

Today: I realize my kinship with the web of life.

Rest Your Dreams on a Little Twig, p. 131

Heart of the Universe

Eternal Heart of the Universe,
I am wrapped in the womb of morning.
I am one with the cooing of doves
and the green of the river's edge.
I am part of the slowly moving water
and the grayness of the wide sky.
All of who I am turns around and walks
toward the center of my being.
I feel a oneness with all of life.

Each of us dwells within you, Womb of Love.
You are the container of our lives.
You are the source of all nourishment,
the safe hold for each of us in our vulnerability.

Today: I am contained within the Heart of the Universe.

Prayers to Sophia, pp. 26–27

Messenger of Love

One way of being a light or a sign
of God's great compassion
is by praying for and with others.
Each morning I name to the Holy One
the significant people of my life.
I also name the groups I will be with
for conferences or retreats in the coming weeks.
In this way, I am reminded of my oneness with others
and of the call to be the messenger of God's love
in all I am and all I do.

Today: I am a messenger of God's love.

The Cup of Our Life, p. 102

May 20

Blessing

May you rest your heartache
in the compassionate arms of the Holy One
and find comfort from this Enduring Love.

May you trust the hidden part of you
where your resilience resides
and remember your inner strength.

May you be gentle and compassionate
with yourself by caring well
for your body, mind, and spirit.

May you recognize when it is time to let go
and move on, doing so when struggle has faded,
and you are ready to allow the past be at rest.

Today: I breathe Love into past hurts and let them go.

Now That You've Gone Home, pp. 177-178

The Inner Radiance

I've experienced some of the strongest light
coming from those who have suffered greatly.
As the darkness breaks their hearts open,
they become ever more vulnerable
and compassionate.

When this happens, walls of resistance,
mental defenses, and tightly held securities
fall away.

Radiant kindness easily spreads
because it has more room to shine.

Today: I observe the light in others.

Little Pieces of Light, p. 60

Find the Good

To find good amid the unwanted aspects of life,
without denying the presence of the unwanted.

To focus on beauty in the little things of life,
as well as being deliberate about the beauties
of art, literature, music, and nature.

To be present to one's own small space of life,
while stretching to the wide world beyond it.

To find something to laugh about in every day,
even when there seems nothing to laugh about.

To be thankful for each loving deed done by another,
no matter how insignificant it might appear.

Today: I find the good where I am.

The Circle of Life, p. 194

MAY 23

Easter Watch

Look for light piercing the gloom.
Receive little joys inside old troubles.
Hold on to love in bleakest of times.
Keep faith alive when filled with doubt.
Accept help from whomever it comes.
Pray in spite of strong resistance.
Laugh amid the tattered tears.

Stand at Easter's emptied tomb.
Remember what the message is.
Shake off what holds you back.
Cast your gaze inside your journey.
Meet the Risen One on the road.
Let renewed hope enter every step.
Watch how Love surprises you.

Today: I will watch for how Love surprises me.

My Soul Feels Lean, p. 145

May 24

Opening

Open our hearts to you, Source of All Souls,
whose love dwells within and among us.

Open us to believe how fully we are welcomed
by you each moment of our lives.

Open us to carry our union with you
to those who are part of our daily encounters.

Open us when we are weary, when we resist,
when we forget, when we doubt, when we are anxious.

Open, open, open us to the journey of love that is ours.

Today: I open my heart to the Source of All Souls.

Prayer Seeds, p. 94

Loved Freely and Fully

Do we ever fully realize how amazing
the love of God is for us?
No matter how seared, smudged, and stained
our life may be, we will always be received
into the merciful embrace of God
when we choose to return.

To be loved freely by God is a tremendous thing.
It is to be received without doubt or hesitation,
to always be regarded as a beloved and cherished one.

Go stand in front of a mirror.
Look fully into your eyes and say, "God is crazy about you."

Today: I believe I am wonder-full in God's eyes.

Inviting God In, p. 63

Stream of Enduring Love

I yearn for a feeling of oneness with you.
I wish I felt driving passion, an insatiable thirst.
Instead, there's just this steady hum of fidelity,
with an occasional flicker of intense longing.

Each day I deliberately place myself
in the midst of your stream of enduring love.
I want so much to feel spiritual refreshment,
to have your divine passion sweep over me
with the power of an energizing waterfall.

I must let go of my desire to desire.
You provide for what I need.
You keep my heart alive in your love.
More than this I do not need.

Today: I quiet the insatiable voice in me.

Prayers to Sophia, p. 90

MAY 27

The Door of Divinity

The story of the Exodus journey exemplifies
the door of divinity as a conduit for spiritual growth.
When the Israelites hurried away from enslavement
in Egypt, they brought with them
an unquenchable thirst for a homeland of their own.

The Door of Love provided access for them
to move toward this goal.

The Great Door never closed to this people
bound together by a desire for liberation.
God's heart remained ajar in spite of their
doubts, hesitations, grumblings, and rebellions.
As they passed through the wilderness,
these wanderers were nourished, forgiven,
guided, and transformed by this faithful Presence.

Today: The Door of Love is open to me.

Open the Door, pp. 22–23

A Gentle Touch

Like a caressing soft breeze
With a ceaseless whisper,
Or a gentle touch on the cheek
Whose imprint remains.
Like a compassionate gaze
Forever remembered,
Or a hand extended openly
Always ready to bestow.
So are you, Unceasing Kindness,
Ever present to our concerns.

Today: I bring a gentle touch to my interactions.

Fragments of Your Ancient Name, June 30

Lessons

While the past cannot be undone,
I can grow from it.
My regrets have motivated me
to change my ways.
I now make an effort
to put people and relationships
before work and productivity.
I am more attentive
to what an older person experiences.
I listen closely when they voice fear and concern,
and decide carefully
before choosing honesty over kindness.

Today: I listen more closely.

Fly While You Still Have Wings, p. 181

May 30

Heart of All Hearts

Teacher of the ways of goodness,
you are hidden in the pockets of daily life
waiting to be discovered.

Heart of Gladness,
Joy that sings in our souls,
the Dancer and the Dance,
you are the Music radiating in our
cherished caches of consolation.

Heart of all Hearts,
the First and Best of all Companions,
you are the Gift secreted in our depths,
connecting us with others.

Today: I rejoice in the Gift secreted in all of us.

Out of the Ordinary, p. 223

Do Something with Love

The Holy One has created each of us
as a wonderful human being
with something special
we are meant to share with our world.

Think of the simple yet significant things
others have done for you
that brought you immense joy
because they were done
with kindness and consideration.

Recognize and accept the beauty
of who you are in God's eyes,
and do something with love today.

Today: I will do something with unconditional love.

God's Enduring Presence, p. 122

Encouraged to Grow

My experience of prayer
has eventually become not so much
a seeking for spiritual benefits
as a rejoicing for the way
God reveals love in my life
and encourages me to grow.

Sometimes there is a pronounced
drawing toward the Other,
but not all prayerful relationships
have this emotional dimension
binding them together.
Nor do they require this affective experience.
What people do need is a conviction
that relationship with God
is an essential part of their existence.

Today: I approach prayer as a source of growth.

Prayer, pp. 24–25

Late-in-Life Friendship

A fresh arrival of friendship,
unexpected upon reaching
seventy, the heart well-calloused
from life's adversity,

An invitation to step out,
to go beyond
where the past limited
the view, to break down
the door nailed shut
by angry demand and loud opinion.

Finally, in these remaining years,
a friend so fine, so good, so true,
so full of dancing spirit
that all the hard years slip away
with barely a whisper.

Today: I open myself to new possibilities.

Fly While You Still Have Wings, pp. 101–102

Those Who Are Searching

Compassionate One,
there are many people in my world
who are searching for something
or someone they treasure.

There are parents filled with heartache
for their lost child.
There are distressed persons
searching for their very self.
There are countless grieving ones
who are looking for a piece of their life
that once gave them happiness.

Bless all who are searching for lost treasure.

Today: I unite in prayer with those who are searching.

Your Sorrow Is My Sorrow, p. 88

Divine Confidante

Where would I be without you
As my confidante and companion?
How would I navigate life's troubles
Without you there to advise me?
Your faithful friendship provides
Vitality, encouragement, confidence,
And endless ingredients of joy.
I learn from you the basic criterion
Of what it means to be a true friend,
Reliant, accessible, and trusting.

Today: I cherish my Companion.

Fragments of Your Ancient Name, February 6

A Simple Container

a simple container
has spoken
in my solitude,
a teacher
and a bringer of wisdom

whispering truths
of an indwelling God
in the container
of my soul

hearkening to
my hidden ability
to be filled
and to pour
from a life
of abundance

reminding me
of necessary boundaries
for nurturing
the sacred space
within me

Today: I strengthen necessary boundaries.

The Cup of Our Life, p. 24

Reassessing Relationships

There were decisions I had to make about
the relationships I carried with me into midlife.
As I looked over the first half of my life,
I saw not only who I had become
but who had been with me in my "becoming."
As I grew clearer about who I was,
I also grew clearer about who I wanted
to have in my life.
I didn't have enough energy anymore
for relationships that constantly drained me
and gave little in return.
Hidden within this process was also
a letting go of an old message of mine
that said I always had to respond
to other people's needs.

Today: I pray to choose wisely.

Dear Heart, Come Home, p. 76

Spiritual Power

Each life influences and affects others
in some way.
The more we see our world
as a vast interconnectedness
of all beings, the more drawn
we will be to compassion
because we will see how much one life
is related to and affected by another.
This spiritual oneness
is at the heart of Christianity.
Christ is the vine, and we are the branches.
The life pulsing through us
is the life of the Holy One giving us spiritual vitality.

Today: I am grateful for spiritual vitality.

The Cup of Our Life, p. 96

Selfless Love

Selfless love is real.
In spite of the horrors of war and other brutal ways
that humans treat one another, love is possible.
Unselfish people reside everywhere.
They love unconditionally,
dedicate themselves to alleviating suffering,
are willing to give their all for another,
intent on being life-givers and spirit-transformers.
They are not do-gooders, holier-than-thou people.
No, this kind of love is seared by trials,
purified by personal growth,
shaped by persistent rededication and self-giving
that goes beyond required duty.

Today: I practice selfless acts of kindness.

Open the Door, p. 150

Will You Be My Friend? Part One

Jesus speaks to me, "Will you be my friend?"

Which is to say:
Will you let me give you my unconditional love?
Will you accept my peace for your tired and worn self?
Will you receive my mercy and forgiveness?
Will you believe in my love when everyone has gone away
and given up on you?
Will you be generous enough to take my love to others
when they need you?
Will you love yourself well and believe in the gifts
I've given to you?

Will you be my friend?

Today: I take these questions to heart.

Out of the Ordinary, p. 218

Will You Be My Friend? Part Two

I listen to the invitation.

I look within and find "yes" answers in
my heart—"Yes" because of dear friends
who have graced my days with love.

Their hearts are plainly flesh and earthen,
yet they touch me with your goodness.
Their hearts are weak and wounded,
yet they mend the torn in me.
Their hearts are tired and troubled,
yet they've time to give me rest.
My friends are loving pathways leading home,
home to where you are, Lover of All Hearts.

Today: I remember friends who are loving pathways.

Out of the Ordinary, pp. 218-219

The Gift of People

People continually come into my life
at just the right moment.
Some come to teach, others to comfort,
some to challenge, and some to affirm.

Some people offer me help when I am struggling
and give direction when I am searching,
and others bring me home to myself
when I have gotten lost in the endless tasks of life.

How much I have learned,
how often I have been comforted,
how many times I have experienced joy,
and how much I have grown
because of the presence of other people in my life.

Today: Each person I meet carries a gift.

The Cosmic Dance, p. 92

June 12

Kinship

Kinship is not just another word for friendship,
community, or kinfolk.
It may be all those things combined and yet
none of those things alone.

Kinship is a rich bondedness that calls
to the deepest parts of ourselves.
It is mutuality of understanding,
a sense of belonging, a union of spirits,
a loving appreciation, and a deep communion
which comes from having known experiences
similar to the person with whom we are bonded.

Kinship confirms our own journey
and gives hope to our struggles.

Today: I reflect on the meaning of kinship in my life.

Praying Our Goodbyes, p. 88

Listening to the Spirit's Movements

Developing an ability to listen
to the Spirit's movements requires practice.
We may never find it easy to do.
Some people are fearful of silence and seek
to fill the space with music, television,
conversation, words, anything but utter stillness.
Others think they cannot pray unless they do away
with the smallest sound around them.
When choosing a time and place of prayer,
it is helpful to have a quiet area,
but this may not always be possible
in our noisy world.
So, instead, we learn to become silent
inside our self and pray amid the external noise
we can neither quell nor control.

Today: I choose to become more at ease with silence.

Prayer, p. 74

Grieving

All-Embracing One,
loneliness threatens to take over my life.
It unravels the fibers of my concentration
and impedes my peace of mind and heart.
Not a day or night goes by without longing
for the companionship and love of my dear one.
When this strong part of grief grabs hold of me,
help me to hear what lies beneath my loneliness:
the depth of love that binds me to this beloved one.
Let me be gentle with the heartache that I feel.

Today: I am gentle with myself.

Now That You've Gone Home, p. 63

Touches of Goodness

Today I am immensely grateful for friends
who come in all shapes and flavors,
who love me as I am with my strengths
and with my never-may-be-transformed foibles.
I am keenly aware of their touches of goodness.
Their warm, considerate elements of care
are comfort and encouragement to me.
They leave my heart more open and alive.
I thank you for every friend I have,
for each one brings me a unique gift of love.

Today: I hold in my heart those whom I call friend.

Prayers to Sophia, p. 38

JUNE 16

The Heart of Mystery

The tones of my life
are often subdued,
muted with paradox,
dimmed
by internal blindness,
hidden
in the folds
of external activity.

Ssshhh,
I hear them calling
in my mind's eye,
calling, calling,
hazily revealing
a place I long to be.

It is none other
than the heart
of Mystery,
the dwelling place
of Home.

Today: I embrace the heart of Mystery.

Rest Your Dreams on a Little Twig, p. 147

JUNE 17

Far-Seeing Eyes

When I greet another person
or any element of the universe
with hospitality,
with welcome and acceptance,
with wonder and awe,
I am bonded. I connect,
and the dance goes on.
It may be the sunset that fills the sky
while I am caught on the freeway;
it may be the first sight and touch
of a baby kitten;
or it may be picking up a broken limb
of an elm tree in the backyard.

Far-seeing moments
can be simple and ordinary,
but they have a way of connecting me
to the essence of life.

Today: I am alert to far-seeing moments.

The Star in My Heart, p. 21

JUNE 18

Those Who Walk with Me

When I was
but a babe
in my spiritual growth,
I followed closely
the wise ones,
the mentors,
the visionaries.

Now that I have grown,
I still need mentors,
wise ones,
and visionaries.

Only now
we walk side by side.

Today: I trust my own path along with the paths of others.

Rest Your Dreams on a Little Twig, p. 53

Love for the Holy One

Does prayer take effort and discipline?
Yes.
Every friendship requires faithful attention
to the relationship.
And, yes, sometimes we have to *work*
at renewing or restoring this bond
because we have a zillion things
that can lead us away from this attentiveness.
But underneath, in our heart of hearts,
the reason we give ourselves
to the effort of prayer is love,
the love that drew us in the first place
into the relationship,
and which is destined to unite us
with the Holy One.

Today: I attend to prayer with love for the Holy One.

Prayer, p. 38

Speaking Openly

From this close friend, Mom gained the ability
to name and talk about her emotional world.

Being able to vocalize interior responses
to life's ups and downs
provides release and support.

This friend spoke openly
about what caused her distress and sorrow.

This openness allowed my mother to be
increasingly unguarded and to more readily
reveal her deeper self.

Today: I speak about my inner world.

Fly While You Still Have Wings, pp. 108–109

Giving Freely

A generous heart freely gives and can live
without some of the material things
we think are desperately needed.
A generous heart is also one that gives freely
of the greater, nonmaterial gifts
such as compassion, understanding,
patience, and forgiveness.
Giving freely means that we give
with no strings attached,
that we give without counting the cost.
In being generous
we do need to take care of ourselves
and give ourselves the gifts of life, love, and time.
Yet, there is such a fine line between being self-centered
and being self-loving and caring well for self.

Today: I am generous with both others and self.

Fresh Bread, p. 140

Spirit of Welcome

Divine Guest,
I lovingly welcome you
with the openness of my entire being.
I desire to receive people who are strangers
with this same spirit of graciousness.
Free my mind when it locks out others.
Disarm my heart of any armor it wears.
I open the door of my heart to you.

Today: I disarm my heart.

Open the Door, p. 159

Wordless Praise

Some moments have no words.
Some relationships have no narration.
They rise silently like the swelling path
of the full moon in a harvest sky,
like the soundless rise and fall
on the breath of one who sleeps gently.

No need to capture, control, contain,
only to be present to the rising,
only to be aware of the silent breathing,
only to be with the unexpected illumination.

It is enough to rest in your love.
It is enough to taste your goodness.
It is enough to call you by name.

Today: It is enough to rest in the Holy One's love.

Prayers to Sophia, pp. 106–107

JUNE 24

Help from Our Friends

How blessed we are if there has been
someone who cared enough not to give up on us.

How thankful we can be if they somehow
brought us to Jesus for greater healing and wholeness.

Great Healer, thank you for all
who brought me to you
in my times of need and hurt.
May I do the same for others
when they are longing to be healed.

Today: I thank someone who has cared for me.

Inviting God In, p. 148

The Kindness of Strangers

The kindness extended to us by strangers
takes us into a larger circle of life.
We become conscious of those we meet each day
as our companions on the pilgrimage of life.
Their caring gestures unite us at a deeper level.
When a gift of helpfulness is extended to us,
it reminds us that the human heart
is a reservoir of love.
When kindness is received with awareness,
we enter into the reality
of being one great family of humanity.

Today: I am a reservoir of love.

Walk in a Relaxed Manner, p. 105

Companion of the Lonely

You hold the hand of lonely ones
As they walk in their dark valleys
Of empty isolation and strayed love.
The widowed, the childless, the lost,
Aged ones never visited, the rejected,
The dying with no one by their side,
Refugees in camps, disabled veterans,
Children abandoned by their parents,
And all those who have not been loved.
We can be your companionship for them.

Today: I reach out to someone who is lonely.

Fragments of Your Ancient Name, November 11

Shelter in the Storm

I know from experience:
standing deep within a linden tree
in a pouring summer rain shower,
one will not get wet.

I know from experience:
sitting very close under scrub oak
in a mountain downpour,
one will not get wet.

I know from experience:
when we draw very near to God's heart,
when we stand deep within God's shelter,
we will not be overcome
with the drenching pain of life.

Today: I draw near to God's shelter.

Praying Our Goodbyes, p. 97

How Many Loves?

How many loves now
have moved across
my heart
leaving permanent marks?

How many loves now
are lost to me
by death
or fickleness
or distance?

How many loves now
press their faces
to the windowpane
of my life
and beg to come in?

Today: I wonder whose love wants to come in.

My Soul Feels Lean, p. 146

Little Pieces of Light

O God,
as I look back on my life
I see many little pieces of light.
They have given me hope and comfort
in my bleak and weary times.

I thank you for the radiance
of a dark sky full of stars,
and for the faithful light of dawn
which follows every turn of darkness.

I thank you for loved ones and strangers
whose inner beacons of light
have warmed and welcomed my pain.

I thank you for your presence in my depths,
protecting, guiding, reassuring, loving.

Today: I marvel at the little pieces of light.

Little Pieces of Light, p. 65

Checking My Motivation

If my motivations come out of "have to,"
guilt, self-affirmation, codependency,
a "fix-it" or problem-solving intention,
or a "redeemer mentality,"
my compassion has too much of me in it
and not nearly enough focus on loving
the one who hurts.

The more I get to know my emotions,
attitudes, compulsions, and desires,
the more transparent
and truly compassionate I will be.

Today: I check on my motivations for what I do.

The Cup of Our Life, p. 104

July 1

A Strong Rainbow

a strong rainbow pours itself out,
bending the eastern sky with glory;
it brings with it a powerful beauty
to soothe my needy heart with hope.

and I do believe I hear the sun
wild with wonder and rejoicing,
laughing at the once-darkened sky
now parted in colored splendor.

I remember then One who came,
who broke our stormy dark apart,
and shook despairing hearts with hope;
this One told truth of things beyond
and gave us more than gold.

Today: The beauty of creation pours over me.

Fresh Bread, p. 78

Summer Stars

A quiet sense of oneness
ripens in me as I gaze
into evening's summer sky.

I behold this endless space
filled with sparkling lights,
speaking of a world unknown,
luring my heart into mystery.

Dancer of the Stars,
I am at home with you
when I view these galaxies
of ageless beauty.

Today: I take time to gaze at the stars and be amazed.

The Circle of Life, p. 136

July 3

A Little Dew Is Enough

One of my fond memories of my childhood
on an Iowa farm is the dew of summer mornings.
The coolness of a new dawn and the grass
would be deliciously wet on my small bare feet.
I remember my father speaking one time
of how his corn crop could be saved in a dry season
if there was enough heavy dew each day.
This moisture on the leaves could be absorbed
by the plant and would help it to survive.

Sometimes we are in a tough spot,
and all we have is a little dew.
Yet, this bit of spiritual moisture or help from God
is enough to see us through until better times.

Today: I am content with a little dew.

Inviting God In, p. 73

Unseen Energy

I sit beneath your tree of life
Receiving the green aliveness.
The unseen energy of your love
Sings in me like photosynthesis
Making music in the happy leaves.
My years with you gather around me
Humming a history of your kindness.
On no day have you ever forsaken me.
In every year you have been there
Greening my life with your grace.

Today: The Holy One's energy of love dwells in me.

Fragments of Your Ancient Name, June 4

My Greatest Blessing

God is, above all else, a being of immense beauty.
It is this beauty that continues to draw us
and enfold us in eternal goodness.
This mysterious Beloved is forever wooing us,
longing for us to be totally immersed in love
of the purest kind.

As I look at my life, I count as my greatest blessing
the gift of God's own essence.
Being able to know this wondrous God of beauty,
being embraced and welcomed home time and again,
all of this is truly powerful.

Today: I am enfolded in eternal goodness.

The Cup of Our Life, p. 133

Inner Garden

Gracious Gardener,
how wondrously you care for my soil.
You send your waters of refreshment.
You fertilize me with your wisdom.
You warm me with your enduring kindness.
You keep drawing me toward your light.
New growth continually sprouts
from the soil of my spiritual garden.
Flowers of creativity bloom.
Herbs of joy flavor my days.
Vegetables of nourishment flourish.
You constantly care for my garden,
weeding it when weaknesses grow tall,
turning the soil when the ground is hard,
comforting and protecting me
when enemies chew on my leaves.

Today: I thank the Gracious Gardener for tending my garden.

Prayers to Sophia, p. 52

Lessons from a Birch Tree

On a trip to Minnesota one summer, I was enthralled
by the white splendor of the birch trees.
I took long walks in the woods and often stopped
to ponder the beautiful groves of white trees on the way.
I was amazed at how their skin-like bark readily peeled off.
My friend told me that the trees could not grow
unless their bark continued to come off,
making room for new growth. She also hastily reminded
        me
as I began to pull off some of the bark,
that if I took the birch bark off before its time,
the tree would be wounded.
The bark had to come off in the tree's own time.
"How like a birch tree I am," I thought,
"only I want the bark to come rolling off all at once."

Today: I am patient with my growth process.

The Star in My Heart, p. 53

The Consolation of Beauty

Beauty consoled and strengthened me
during the countless times my legs and feet hurt
from walking and my shoulders pained
from carrying my backpack.
The Camino's loveliness uplifted me
when my body sagged from illness.
Beauty brought back contentment
when I whined about unsanitary bathrooms.
The natural splendor around me gave me hope
when my hungry soul longed for a touch
of enthusiasm.

Always the many forms of beauty on the Camino
reached out to me, asking nothing more
than that I embrace their gifts.

Today: I receive the beauty of creation.

Walk in a Relaxed Manner, pp. 117–118

The Blessing of the Ordinary

I don't know about you,
but something in me hesitates
to trust revelations of God
when they are too ordinary.
I like to think that God is mostly revealed
in something "big" or outstandingly beautiful,
like the Swiss Alps.
The truth is that God is mostly revealed
in those nearest to us, wherever we are.
It is *how* we look for God, what we expect,
that makes the difference.
Let us give up the "high mountains
and vast oceans" as our major searching places
and come home to our simple lives.

Today: I look among the ordinary for divine revelation.

Inviting God In, p. 42

Attention

a small frog
floating, splayed out, waiting,
all of her body in the pond
except her goggled eyes,
round buttons of attention,
rising above the clear water

a small frog,
looking, I realize, at me
while I look at her,
both curious
about the other's presence

a small frog
silently attentive,
calling me back to stillness
until I sit without purpose

Today: I return to stillness.

My Soul Feels Lean, p. 109

Serenade of the Song Sparrow

Outside my small cabin
hidden among the birch and pines
on a northern Minnesota bluff
a song sparrow opens the dawn
with the first of an all-day
serenade.

Cheerful and clear it awakens
not only my sleepy eyes
but my drowsy heart
dulled with its endless effort
to meet the ego's requirements.

Today: I listen for what wants to be heard.

Prayer Seeds, p. 137

The Magnificence of Creation

No matter how pressed my life is
or how fraught with difficulty,
I do eventually wake up.
My desire to be aware is restored
most often through finally stopping,
or being stopped,
by the sheer magnificence of creation.
I have been ambushed by the power of the moon,
held captive by fireflies dancing at dusk,
bowled over by wobbly white shoots
beneath a rock pushing their way out to life,
moved to tears by the sight of a small finch
falling from the roof.
I have lain on the picnic table and gazed
at the stars in sheer ecstasy
until I thought the only option for my heart
was to die at that moment.

Today: I rejoice at the magnificence of creation.

The Cosmic Dance, p. 31

JULY 13

Renew My Strength

God of Strength,
who calls forth eagles
to bend wings in adoration,
who sends forth eagles
to wing wide in praise,
I am in need of your strength.
Carry me on your loving wings.
Renew my strength.
Give me the energy for the going
and create in me
an openness to future flying.
Great God of eagles' hearts,
I want to trust that you will bear me up,
that you will support me.
I look to you to renew my strength
just as surely as eagles' wings
are wide in the sky.

Today: I am carried on the wings of divine strength.

Praying Our Goodbyes, p. 110

Azalea Leaves

light raindrops
        rinse the tired azalea leaves

slowly washing off
        the dreary residue
        of a hot summer's glaze

not enough moisture
        to reach
        the parched roots

but every droplet
        cheers the slaked plant,
        reminding it of better days
        when rain fell steadily

Today: Divine love rains upon my parched roots.

My Soul Feels Lean, p. 45

July 15

Perception

Interior solitude cleared a space in me
for contemplation.
My eyes took in everything with wonder.
The experience was like looking through
the lens of an inner camera—
my heart was the photographer.
Colors and shapes took on nuances
and depths never before noticed.
Each piece of beauty appeared to be framed:
weeds along roadsides,
hillsides of harvested fields
with yellow and green stripes,
layers of mountains with lines of thick mist.
Everything revealed itself
as something marvelous to behold.
Each was a work of art.

Today: I look at life through the lens of my heart.

Walk in a Relaxed Manner, p. 174

The Gift of Trees

Trees have a special way
of connecting me to the cosmic dance.
The leap of life fills my spirit
when I spend time with them.
I sense a dynamic energy there
waiting to be received by my spirit.
One morning when I was attending
a seminar in Louisville, I walked by
a pine tree whose arms were filled
with fresh spring growth.
The lime-green shoots
were a beauty to behold.
I stood there with the pine tree,
opened my hands,
and asked to receive the energy
and the beauty of that life-filled tree.

Today: I receive energy from nature.

The Star in My Heart, p. 25

JULY 17

Lily of the Valley

Such powerful fragrance
From one tiny humble flower.
A whiff of its intense sweetness
Absorbs my complete attention.
So it is with the divine essence.
One whiff, one brief encounter,
Only this much is necessary
To restore spiritual balance.
Remembrance of this aroma
Lingers long and lovingly with me.

Today: I regain spiritual balance.

Fragments of Your Ancient Name, May 27

Sabbath Time

The only sounds
breaking the immense quiet
are crickets humming
and the first yawns
of robins and cardinals.

My soul awakens with ease,
cradled in meditation,
sung to by your stillness,
Silent Sentinel of my Soul.

And I am delivered
for a while
from the torture
of endless schedules
and the deafening noise
of my own desires.

Today: I set aside noisy demands for a while.

Prayers to Sophia, pp. 80-81

Inspired by the Dawn

I loved best of all the mornings
we started out in the dark.
On those days we walked silently under the stars,
with the countryside serenely quiet before dawn.
Gradually, the first bird began to sing.
Eventually, as light seeped into the darkness,
we turned around from time to time
so we could catch the rising sun.
Sometimes we stopped and stood in awe as daybreak
spread color across the eastern horizon.
One early dawn we were awestruck
as we walked between the two companions of our planet:
the red ball of sun rising over our shoulder
through the thick mist in the east
and the full moon hanging elegantly before us
in the west.

Today: I face the east and give praise for the dawn.

Walk in a Relaxed Manner, p. 122

Longevity

Flowers last
a long, long time
if they have
what they need.

Why is it
that I neglect
myself?

I need to feed
on beauty,
walk more often
under starlight,
listen to the wind,
and rest my weariness.

Then my flowers
will last
a long, long time.

Today: I tend to what feeds my spirit.

Radiant Presence

Stars are used in many places in scripture
to proclaim the wonder and power of God.
The vastness of the sky and its stars
called to those who were drawn to the divine.
I can easily understand why this is so.
I don't think I've ever stood silently
beneath a star-filled sky
and not felt drawn to the holy Presence.
There is an immediate sense of how small I am
and how large the universe is.
But there is more: I sense a closeness
in spite of my smallness.
I sense an attraction and a yearning for mystery
that far outreaches my rational mind.
My whole being is filled with an "ah,"
and I find myself wanting to kneel
before beauty and mystery of the Creator.

Today: I am at home with mystery.

Inviting God In, p. 30

Carrying Stories

The constant, small ripples of water
splashing against the rocks,
each miniature wave carrying a story,
some from the ancient glaciers
and some from this present age of mine.
The rain-swollen clouds hold our tales of life,
and drop them into the expansive lake
year after year, absorbing
them into the one Great Story.

Today the ripples invite me to listen intently,
to find within them my own narrative:
the womb-like waters of a nine-month gestation,
the gush and push of a small, unknown self
into a world that has grown me
into the person I now am.

Today: I identify the narrative of my life.

Prayer Seeds, p. 29

July 23

Turning Inward

On the mesa, insignificant things of life
sink into oblivion. The self is forced
to let go of what is unimportant
as the journey itself takes the pilgrim forward.
All else is forgotten as one plods along,
mile after flat, hot mile,
enveloped in silent solitude
that provides growth.
The miles and miles of walking
evoke the emptying of self
so that life is seen with renewed clarity
and all that one values
is put into its proper place.

Today: I observe needs that should be put into their proper place.

Walk in a Relaxed Manner, pp. 178–179

The Value of Just Being There

Influenced by my production-oriented Western culture,
I have often underestimated the value of "just being
there."
Sometimes there's a voice in me
that insists I have to *do* something.
This voice questions the effectiveness of presence.
Is it enough just to listen?
Is it sufficient to sit by the bedside?
Shouldn't I bring something?
Can't I say something that will make a difference?
Something deep inside keeps trying to convince me
that if I just know the "right" things to say or do,
then both the hurting one and I will feel better.
Sometimes words do help; many times, "just being there"
is most comforting and helpful.

Today: I practice "just being there."

Inviting God In, p. 113

July 25

Recovering Joy

Why is joy a neglected part of prayer?
Most of us surely do enough complaining
and beseeching of God
when things don't go our way.
How can we balance our requests and wants
with thanksgiving and joy?
One way I've found to nurture
a spirituality of gladness
is by remembrance.
Each day before closing my eyes for sleep,
I look back over the day that is ending.
No matter how troublesome the day has been,
I recover my joy by asking,
"What is one thing in this day for which I can be glad?"

Today: I find one thing for which to be glad.

God's Enduring Presence, p. 47

Sower of Seeds

O Sower of Seeds,
did you always see
this gift of green
that was hiding in me?

O Sower of Seeds,
how came you to prize
the beauty within
that I hid from my eyes?

O Sower of Seeds,
the husk has been broken;
all praise to you
for helping me open.

Today: I unite with the Sower of Seeds.

Fresh Bread, p. 68

Community

Branches touch.
Limbs assure one another,
"I'm here."

No matter how fierce the storm,
"I'm here."

In spite of how jagged
and torn the branches,
"I'm here
beside you through the long
turbulent nights.

I'll reach to connect
with you
in the wildest of winds.
Be assured of my presence.
Have confidence.
I'm here."

Today: I have confidence that I am not alone.

My Soul Feels Lean, p. 151

Walk in a Relaxed Manner

Walking in a relaxed manner is challenging.
There was just too much "hurry" built up in us
through the years to keep us from instantly
changing our ways.
Whenever we thought we were well established
in our new attitude and behavior,
one of us would want to go further
than we originally agreed.
At other times one of us would pick up the pace
or start voicing concern about whether or not
we'd find room at the next refugio.
We had to constantly give our attention
to going slowly in spirit as well as in body.
It took effort to be present to the new approach
we were birthing and growing as we walked.

Today: I walk in a relaxed manner.

Walk in a Relaxed Manner, p. 57

Companions of Growth

My companions of growth have been diverse,
but all have had one common characteristic:
each trusted in my potential for growth.
I would never have found the key to my inner garden
had they not believed in the possibilities
yet to come alive in my undeveloped self.
These companions challenged me to see
the parts of my self encumbered by my ego.
They gave me courage to seek and find
the veiled realm of my authentic self.
Others can help us open the door to our heart.
We need them to teach us how to pray,
to encourage us to find and use our personal talents,
to challenge us to expand our minds and hearts,
to assure our efforts.

Today: I am grateful for my companions of growth.

Open the Door, pp. 29-30

Restoration in the Garden

Quiet communion with the garden
revives the peace and tranquility
that all too easily slip away from me.
The garden's fragrances, colors, and shapes
comfort my inner weariness.
Its bounty feeds not only my body
but also my soul.
As I stoop, kneel, sit, and stand
among the garden's verdant vegetation,
I forget about the busy things
that seemed so important to me.
The garden becomes a sanctuary
of repose and promise,
a graced place that allows my body and spirit
room to breathe freshness.
Here in the garden I am reminded
of my communion with all that lives.

Today: I allow my peace to be restored.

The Circle of Life, p. 122

Another Form of Eucharist

Eucharist comes in many forms.
Yesterday at dawn I stepped
onto the round, white stones
of Lake Michigan's vast shore;
I felt the deepest communion
with all that exists, especially
with the One who woos my heart.

Today, as the retreat house bell
calls the women to come and receive,
I stand before the full-bodied,
incandescent maple tree, sunshine
illuminating its golden leaves
like a host held high in the blue sky.
I stand in creation's communion line,
bow my head, open my heart,
and receive Eucharist once again.

Today: I bow my head and open my heart.

Prayer Seeds, p. 156

August 1

Serving through Our Work

Work changes into service when we view it
as more than something that has to be done,
when it becomes a way for our authentic self
to transmit integrity, kindness, and justice.

A huge amount of work in our world
begs to be done with an attitude of care.
Let us be of service to others
with our strengths *and* our limitations,
trusting that God will take the best
of who we are and bless others with it.

Today: I approach my work as service.

Open the Door, pp. 148–149

Discipleship

To follow Jesus in discipleship
means that sometimes I will be rejected
and misunderstood.
I may not see results in ministry,
and I will need to give
when nothing seems to be returned.
"To follow" is to serve
when the body and the spirit are weary
and to never know what lies ahead.
"To follow" is to live with mystery
and to walk in faith,
knowing that we are deeply loved.

Today: I will "follow" and walk in faith.

Fresh Bread, p. 118

The Value of Receiving

I myself have had to discover the value
in being the receiver and not always the giver.
I have had to learn that when I allow
someone else to do a kindness for me,
my receptivity becomes a gift for them.

I usually gain a sense of satisfaction and self-worth
when I help others in any kind of loving way.
So if I balk at or refuse to receive another's kindness,
I am, in a sense, denying them the pleasure
they could have by tending to my needs.

Today: I remember to receive as well as to give.

God's Enduring Presence, p. 41

Misjudging Others

Those who observed Jesus as he preached
and healed questioned how he could have
such wisdom and skills when he was
"only the carpenter's son."

Do I ignore certain people because
their work seems menial or insignificant?
Can I be more respectful of everyone who works,
regardless of the nature of their efforts?

Little do I know which person,
famous or unknown, is doing their work
in a way that transforms their heart,
thus bringing more love and goodness
into our world.

Today: I respect each person who enters my life.

God's Enduring Presence, p. 63

AUGUST 5

Lighten Up

Help me to enter into
the joyful dimensions of my work.
Let me not be so involved and serious
about my work
that I miss the many pleasures and joys
that are inherent in it.
Lighten me up when I am feeling my work's heaviness.
May I remember that I need balance in my life,
that laughter and leisure are essential
for my total health.
Take me to sources of zest and enthusiasm
without hesitation or guilt.

Today: I lighten up and laugh more.

Out of the Ordinary, p. 131

Consecrating Our Tasks

Too often we judge ourselves or others
by what we do rather than the attitude
with which we do our work.

Work is more than making money,
having prestige, and finding success.

It is an opportunity to use and share
our God-given talents and to minister
to the Christ who dwells in other people.

Today: I put sincere "heart" into what I do.

Inviting God In, p. 101

A Love of Life

Lover of Life,
I have forgotten what it is like to be fully alive.
I have become a functional, productive, serious adult.
What grasps my enthusiasm, my love of life,
and drags it down to the cellar and locks it up?
What causes me to neglect my deepest needs?
What leads me to be overly giving and responsible?
How can I let your creative, invigorating presence
be more fully alive and active in my life?

Today: I get reacquainted with my love of life.

Prayers to Sophia, p. 98

Calling Back to Life

Has kindness or generosity withered
into daily nagging and constant complaining?
Has hope slumped into relentless discouragement?
Has patience shriveled into harsh language?
Has prayer dried up from neglect?
Has peace of mind dissolved into anxiety?
Now is the time to face whatever needs
some renewed verve and vitality.
Call it back to life with the same confidence
that Ezekiel had in that valley of dry bones.
Remember it was the movement of God's Spirit
that came upon the dry bones and restored flesh to them.
So, too, with what awaits enlivening in us.

Today: I call back to life what needs enlivening.

God's Enduring Presence, p. 25

August 9

Compassion and Kindness

Compassionate One,
when I am irritated and discouraged
by how my loved one responds
or does not respond,
fill me with compassion and kindness.
When memories of unpleasant experiences
of the past return,
assist me in extending forgiveness.
Help me, also, to be kind to myself,
to not deny the struggles.
Soothe my sore spirit
when I find the days especially difficult.

Today: My compassion is strengthened through prayer.

May I Walk You Home?, pp. 23–24

AUGUST 10

On Loan

Deep down we know that all is on loan to us.
Life does change and sometimes so quickly.
Accidents happen, disease spreads,
storms come, aging continues,
jobs terminate, mistakes occur.
All of life is filled with loss and with letting go.
For the one who believes that all is on loan,
this is to be expected.
Not that this expectation cripples
the spirit of joy.
Just the opposite is true;
the present moment is treasured
and enjoyed all the more
because it is so precious and fleeting.

Today: Life is meant to be enjoyed.

Praying Our Goodbyes, p. 51

Singing for Joy

Sing for the delight of pure joy,
of laughter and unmitigated fun,
dance suffused with playfulness
and passionate engagement with life.

Sing for the heart's secluded secrets
snuggled in unpretentious corners,
secrets waiting to be called forth,
aching for the confidence of words.

Sing for the mystery held in the soul,
the melody born in every person;
sing for this resonating beauty,
the presence of indwelling harmony.

Today: I hum a favorite song during the day.

Prayer Seeds, p. 152

Spirit of Putter

Slow me from the frantic pace.
Help me halt the constant pressure
Of getting the hurried things done.
Let me dawdle the day away,
Ease into the morning snail-like.
Savor what I usually zoom by,
Tinker with stuff here and there.
And at the end of the idle day,
Let me be content with doing nothing
Except enjoying my time with you.

Today: I will be content.

Fragments of Your Ancient Name, May 29

Doing Our Best Each Day

We all live with mystery.
No one can predict
how what is happening now
will influence and affect the future.
All we know is that we are asked
to trust that our loving efforts each day
are of value in the eyes of God.

We are asked to have faith
that our lives will bear fruit.
It is not an easy thing to believe,
especially if our lives are filled with pain,
struggle, or grief,
or a sense of meaninglessness.

Today: The results of my efforts are in God's hands.

Inviting God In, p. 111

Handling Positive Comments

I grew up in a family where adults believed
the less you praised someone the better,
lest that person become too proud.
But praise is actually an essential component
of positive human development.
We all need it.

True praise, not false flattery,
helps us believe in and accept the talents
and virtuous qualities God has bestowed on us.
How else would the Holy One praise us
except by speaking through the sincere comments
coming from others?

Today: I remember to praise someone.

God's Enduring Presence, p. 33

An Attitude of Discipleship

Because of the attitude of discipleship
we can go to our tasks knowing God dwells with us,
strengthening and encouraging us.
The yoke is easier and the burden lighter
because it is for the Holy One that we are at work.
It is this love that gives life to our ministry.
It is our great desire to share this love
that energizes our work.

Be especially aware of your feelings
about your work, its ups and downs.
Notice how you let those feelings
influence your thinking and actions.
Look often at why you do your work
and where your focus is.

Today: My work is done in union with the Spirit of Love.

Fresh Bread, p. 120

Faith Is about Trusting

Faith is about trusting
without seeing the whole picture.
As much as we yearn to know
and understand fully,
we can only see a small part
of who God is
and why our life unfolds as it does.
No matter how much we pray and study,
we cannot fully explain the divine mystery
that lies within and beyond us.
All that is required is that we daily
place our hand in the Holy One's hand
with confidence and walk lovingly in life.

Today: I place my hand in the Holy One's hand.

God's Enduring Presence, p. 49

Inner Resiliency

A cottonwood tree that stands tall and lean
by Lake Michigan has taught me
about responding to unwanted losses.
Each time I visit Racine, Wisconsin,
I stand for quite a long while
looking at the tree
that I call my sentinel of strength.

A long swath of stripped-off bark
along one side of the trunk bears evidence
of its having been struck by lightning.
I often ask the tree, "How have you endured?
What is your secret?"

Each time I hear one word: "Resiliency."

Today: I am aware of my inner resiliency.

Boundless Compassion, p. 71

Overburdened

Immersed in my intensity,
bludgeoned with responsibility,
I focus on the thousand items
shouting at me from my precarious perch
where I wheeze with self-pity.

"Lighten up,"
your graced voice suggests
as I struggle in the net
of my desolate self-destruction.

Where did I develop the notion
that I could do it all?
When did I smugly decide
I could handle everything
without you by my side?

Today: I let go of unrealistic expectations.

Prayers to Sophia, pp. 56–57

The Violet

The simplicity
of a violet
sings in my soul.

The push
to be productive,
the rush
to be responsible,

all this fades
in the beauty
of the violet.

I struggle again
to be free
from seductive lies
telling me
to crowd my days
with success.

Today: I do not let my ego deceive me.

Rest Your Dreams on a Little Twig, p. 95

Inner Seeing, Outer Being

When I stop the hurry in my life,
pause for leisure and be-ing time,
I can much more easily
join in Sophia's dance of life.

I can look upon all of life
with the vision that it is sacred,
helping me to reverence and cherish
people, creatures, and elements
of the universe.

My external senses, as well as my inner ones,
such as intuition and emotion,
facilitate the process of joining
my outer world with my inner world,
giving me deeper vision and clarity of life.

Today: I lessen the hurry in my life.

The Star in My Heart, p. 25

AUGUST 21

The Spirit at Work

No matter what form of paid or volunteer work,
whether actively engaged outside the home
or in it, the most valuable gift we bring
to this labor is our self.
The more we open the door to our depths
and learn from what we find there,
the greater spiritual richness
we are able to bring to others.
We go forth humbly, not hiding behind
the careful defense of our persona.
We set out with the power of the Holy One
alive and resilient in us, a union that strengthens
our sense of self and our ability
to bring our inner goodness into our occupations.

Today: I bring my goodness into the work of this day.

Open the Door, pp. 147–148

Reawakening

imagine the first time
you opened your eyes
and saw a human face

imagine the first time
you heard the sound
of your own name

imagine the first time
you looked at a flower
and smelled the fragrance

now take it all in again
as if today
is your last day

Today: I do not take anything for granted.

The Cosmic Dance, p. 39

Source of Amazement

I am sometimes seized by wonder
At daily marvels large and small,
Birthing, living, loving, playing,
Things amazing, awesome, splendid.
They zap my overly full mind into alertness
And refresh my dull connection with you.
Thank you for the regular reminders
That come sailing out of nowhere.
These gifts let me slow my harried breath
And cause me to wipe happy tears of wonder.

Today: I notice something that amazes me.

Fragments of Your Ancient Name, May 13

The Playground of God

Leisure is more than just not doing anything.
It is intentionally enjoying life
without having to be functional or productive.
When we are experiencing leisure,
we often do not have anything to show for it
except a happy heart or a spirit
that relishes time spent alone or with others.

Focus on wonder.
Try to see the world through the eyes of a child
and discover what happiness really is.

Today: I look with the eyes of a child.

May I Have This Dance?, p. 114

AUGUST 25

In the Green Forest

Here in the green forest
I know a presence
bigger than myself,
stronger than
the ponderosa pines.

Here in the whispering forest
I hear a voice
softer than the sighing
of swaying branches.

Here in the dark forest
I see a truth
shining through the boughs,
telling me
I am not alone.

Today: I listen to the deeper things of life.

Rest Your Dreams on a Little Twig, p. 111

A Garden Reflection

My spirit breathes in the mystery
as I take in the wonderment.
It sighs with contentment.
The garden's potential to nurture life
is just what my heart needs.
I gain inner strength from observing
the garden's resilient and prolific abilities.
I rejoice in the signs of growth before me,
humbly acknowledging that I cannot force
the garden to grow.
I am only a caretaker of what is produced.

Today: I humbly rejoice in my spiritual growth.

The Circle of Life, p. 121

Unwanted Tasks

Doing things we do not want to do,
cleaning a house, going to work,
packing a suitcase, tending a child,
flossing teeth, telling the truth,
preparing a meal, forgiving a hurt,
weeding the garden, buying food.

How to savor what floats between
the unwanted things: the trickles of
kindness, the sudden entrance of a thought
settling our inner disturbance,
the chance meeting of a blue sky, a kiss
breathing through body and soul,
the unexpected hour of free space
allowing time to unburden a schedule.

Today: I find something to savor amid the unwanted.

Prayer Seeds, p. 138

August 28

Surprise

Just about the time I get dogmatic,
Certain that I know it all,
You upend what I thought was fact.
Just about the time I drown in tears,
You enter in with unmitigated joy.
Just about the time I yawn in monotony,
You come dancing in with a lively step.
Just about the time I think I know you,
You turn up and show another side of yours.
And there I am, surprised again.

Today: I wait upon the God of Surprises.

Fragments of Your Ancient Name, September 8

Bringing a Blessing

Teacher and Healer,
you brought the gift of yourself
to those who benefited from your work.
You touched them with wellsprings of love.
Remind me each day to do the same.
Consecrate all I do today
so my service to others brings a blessing.
I open the door of my heart to you.

Today: I live in a way that brings kindness to others.

Open the Door, p. 149

Prayer of Inner Peace

Restore my perception of the inherent joy
that awaits me in each day
if only I turn toward you with a recognition
of your vibrant energy moving through me.

Awaken me to a keener awareness
of your light-filled presence within my being,
especially when life fills with shadows of sadness
and the cloudiness of concerns.

Show me how you are dwelling
in those places of my life where I've forgotten
to welcome you with an open heart
of acceptance and hospitality.

Today: I return often to my inner sanctuary.

Prayer Seeds, p. 160

August 31

The Work of Our Hands

Think of what you accomplish in one day
with the use of your hands.
Imagine your life if you did not have
these two magnificent gifts.
How different life would be
without the mobility and dexterity
of our hands.

These helpful parts of the body
symbolize various aspects of "work,"
including service, hospitality,
giving and receiving, caring and generosity.

Today: I appreciate the work of my hands.

God's Enduring Presence, p. 113

SEPTEMBER 1

Holy Mystery

Mystery penetrates every aspect
of my life with you, Divine Secret.
I cannot know or understand where
the call to be yours will take me.
I do not need to know,
even though I *want* to know.
All that is required is that I trust you
with my life.
Wrap your love around me
so completely
that I will readily give you my "yes."

Today: Divine Secret wraps love around me.

Out of the Ordinary, p. 133

El Shaddai

El Shaddai, God of the mountains,
The strong, noble, powerful one,
Whom Abraham and Sarah
Called by name in their prayer.
You are also "the breasted one,"
Spoken to by prayerful ancients.
I call upon you, too, in my need,
To empower me in uncertainty,
To embolden me in fearfulness,
To strengthen me in weakness.

Today: I look to El Shaddai for strength.

Fragments of Your Ancient Name, September 21

The Pilgrim Journey

To be a pilgrim is to be willing
to live with the mystery
of what will happen
both interiorly and exteriorly
as one walks day after day
toward the destination of a sacred site.
What happens inside cannot be planned
or mapped out in the same way
that the physical route is mapped.
Becoming a pilgrim means
there are no maps of the heart.
One simply holds onto the hand
of the Great Pilgrim
and travels with hope that one day
the spiritual benefits of the road
will reveal themselves and be understood.

Today: I shift my interior focus and live with mystery.

Walk in a Relaxed Manner, p. 40

September 4

Knowing

Holy Mystery,
we come to an awareness
of how close you are to us
when we are swept into a place of "knowing"
that lies beyond our rational control.
Today we remember and bring our gratitude
for those quickly fleeting glimpses
of our deep and strong unity with you.
We turn again to draw strength
from the unexplainable sureness
of your abiding love.
Remind us of this glimpse on the days
when our minds and hearts seem far from you.

Today: I recall fleeting glimpses of God's Presence.

Prayer Seeds, p. 42

September 5

Guidance

Trusted Guide,
you are my Mentor, my Inspiration,
my Home of good choices and decisions.
You help me to search with confidence
as I find my way to inner peace.

Teach me how to hear your voice,
to be aware of what is in my mind and heart,
to attend to your wisdom in those around me,
to acknowledge my intuitions
and ponder my dreams,
to listen to the earth and all of life,
for in each piece of my existence
you are guiding me.

Today: I listen for guidance.

Prayers to Sophia, p. 46

September 6

Disguised Blessings

Some of our greatest blessings have been
difficult situations, uncomfortable ones
we wanted to throw out of our lives
as quickly as possible.
Sometimes our greatest pain holds a gift for us
that is hidden for a long, long time.
The blessing is disguised amid the turmoil,
confusion, heartache, and struggle.
Sometimes we are unable to accept the blessing
because we are still too hurt, too angry,
too grieved, too overwhelmed to receive it.
It is only much later that we see the gift
that has come from what we thought
would destroy our happiness forever.

Today: I ponder my disguised blessings.

The Cup of Our Life, pp. 127–128

More Than Self-Reliance

When I am in situations that are difficult,
I often hear God saying to me:
"Don't rely only on yourself.
I will come into your life
if you will invite and welcome me there.
The two of us together can do much more
for this situation than just you, by yourself.
Trust me to be there for you."

It's not that I always get what I want
when I knock on that divine door,
but I can always count on receiving what I need.

Today: I rely on more than just myself.

Inviting God In, p. 58

Sophia

Sophia,
You are the Wisdom of God.
You are the Whirl of the Spirit.
You are the Intimate Connection.
You are the Star in my Heart.

Open me to the radiance of your presence,
to the guidance of your companionship,
to the compassion of your indwelling,
to the lighting of your blessed vision.

Bless the frailty of my weak places.
Strengthen my ability to dwell in darkness,
for it is there that your deepest secrets are revealed.

Today: I invoke Sophia's wisdom.

The Star in My Heart, p. 1

September 9

Tapping Lovingly

At night
with two pillows propped
behind me,
out of nowhere
in the middle of turning
a page, I sigh,
realizing I am at peace,
happy and content.

I pause in my reading,
put the book down,
aware of something undefined.

I close my eyes,
breathe in
what feels like someone
tapping lovingly
on the door of my heart.

Today: I am alert to the Holy One's tapping.

My Soul Feels Lean, p. 111

SEPTEMBER 10

A Time to Dance

Prayer keeps hope active and restores life
to the dead bones of our dreams.
Prayer is meant to be much more
than just a storehouse or a reservoir
where we get filled up so that we can work harder.
This concept only reinforces our compulsive
work ethic.

Regaining our energy and vitality may happen
when we seek time apart with God,
but we seek that time for the sake of the relationship,
not because we want more success in our work.
Prayer is a time to dance with our Divine Partner,
to let the Beloved One take the lead
and to enjoy the true delight and source of life
that God is for us.

Today: I dance with my Divine Partner.

May I Have This Dance?, pp. 12-13

Intention

Having a conscious *intention* to be at prayer
is vital if we are to come home to that inner place
of unity and peace to which God invites us.
Intention means to be right here, right now.
Before beginning to pray,
we deliberately set as our purpose
that of being in relationship with God.
Intention implies a conscious choice of
remembering this beloved presence.
We intentionally move our awareness
toward our deepest center,
even if our wandering mind and listless heart
challenge our desire to do so.

Today: I intentionally unite with the Holy One.

Prayer, p. 66

She Who Is

Finally you are being acknowledged,
Not as He Who Is but She Who Is.
Another face of divinity to guide us,
A feminine movement of aliveness,
A divine, relational, knowable presence.
You draw us into sacred community
And challenge troubling exclusivity
With your invitation of partnership.
You choose to reveal yourself to us
Through silent, intuitive glimpses.

Today: "She Who Is" invites me inward.

Fragments of Your Ancient Name, October 19

Dance of the Universe

Passionate Presence,
dance your vibrant life within me.
Leap and bound joyfully through me.
I yearn to be centered and alive
so I can join the dance of the universe.
Help me to enter into greater oneness
with each and every part of creation.
Fill me with your enlivening vision
until I fully know that I am a sister
with all that roams, and wings, and swims.

Today: My heart dances with vibrant life.

Prayers to Sophia, p. 28

SEPTEMBER 14

The Ordinariness of Life

I simply cannot imagine a prayer,
a poem, or a reflection
not being connected
with the commonness of life,
for it is there I experience
who I am and how God is with me.

As I seek to relate to God through prayer,
I do not step out of the reality of my life.
Rather, I step into it more fully
with a keen sense that this is where
my spiritual transformation occurs.

Today: I pray within the ordinariness of my day.

Out of the Ordinary, pp. xiv–xv

Planting a Seed

Each year I observed my mother planting
her large garden with vegetable and flower seeds
while my father sowed the fields of black earth
with kernels of corn, soybeans, and oats.
Over the summer I enjoyed watching this
come to life, amazed at the greening
and growth emerging from the plantings.
When autumn arrived,
happiness skipped inside of me
as we gathered the garden's abundance
and loaded the heaping wagons
with golden grain from the fields.
All this coming from what was once
small, nondescript seeds.
What a truly wondrous process
within a seed,
when it is cared for and tended.

Today: Each prayer I utter is like a seed being planted.

Prayer Seeds, p. ix

Listening to My Soul

Guardian of my Deepest Self,
I need only to be still, to listen,
not only to falling leaves
and the gentle wind;
I need to listen to my soul,
too long neglected
while I bowed to the wild cries
of my greedy culture,
ever ravenous
for my undivided attention:
Do more. Buy more.
See more. Be more. Go more.

I am weary
with feeding this huge mouth
that devours my soul.

Today: I listen to my soul.

Prayers to Sophia, p. 58

SEPTEMBER 17

Surprising Surrender

Fireflies danced in the forest
while the summer stars
wove wondrous patterns
in the early night sky.

How good it felt
in that fleeting space
of starlit night;
how easy, then, to surrender.

On that starlit night
something in me gave way,
opened up, let go,
and in that moment of surrender,
Sophia brought me home again.

Today: My heart opens wider.

The Star in My Heart, pp. 88-89

SEPTEMBER 18

The Eyes of Faith

Because we are pilgrims
whose homeland is not here,
we journey, search, travel, discover,
live with mystery, doubt, and wonder.
We see dreams come true, see hopes alive.
We see dreams dashed, see hopes die.
We start over again—with people, work, prayer,
our whole life, all the days of our life.
It is the way of the human spirit.

The journey inside always has the aura
of mystery and challenge
because when we travel inward,
we can see only with the eyes of faith.

Today: I approach transitions with the eyes of faith.

Praying Our Goodbyes, p. 46

September 19

To Bless

Anyone and anything that brings good or God-ness
into our lives is a blessing.
To bless is to bring the touch of God,
the touch of love and goodness,
to another by our presence, as well as by our actions.
Blessings are a greeting from God, saying,
"I care about you. I desire what will be for your good.
You are dear to my heart.
I want your life to be filled with love."

Blessings are not always immediate,
"feel good" sorts of things.
Sometimes these blessings come disguised
in the pain, struggle, and hardship
of the unwanted parts of our lives.
It is only later, with hindsight,
that we look and see what a gift
those times and events were for us.

Today: My kindness brings a touch of God to others.

The Cup of Our Life, p. 118

Connecting with Divine Love

What happens in our prayer time
will naturally affect the rest of our lives.
Gradually we will become more deeply aware
of God's presence in the everyday world around us.
We cannot isolate our spiritual life
from the rest of our life,
for it is in our day-to-day situations
that we experience our personal transformation
toward wholeness.
When we enter our time of prayer
we bring our life and our work with us.
We do so in order to connect with God,
to renew that relationship so it permeates our whole life.

Today: I become more aware of God's presence.

May I Have This Dance?, p. 4

September 21

Breath of Life

Could I live without you?
No more than I can exist
Without oxygen for my lungs.
You sustain my pulse of life,
Both internally and externally.
Each breath of your love
Rejuvenates my spirit.
You sustain my daily rhythm
Of being a loving presence
In all I am and all I do.

Today: My breath becomes a prayer.

Fragments of Your Ancient Name, May 1

SEPTEMBER 22

An Invitation

Darkness sometimes invites us
to reconsider our notion of God.
Our understanding and our metaphors
for the divine being
may be too limiting for our adult lives.
Perhaps we are being stretched
into considering the dark One of the womb,
as well as the divine One of the light.
"Even darkness to you is not dark,
and night is as clear as the day" (Ps 139:12).

Today: I consider my notion of who God is.

Little Pieces of Light, pp. 40-41

SEPTEMBER 23

Wordless Longing

There is an "ache" in autumn
that is also within each one of us.
This ache is the deep stillness
of a late September morning
when mist covers the land
and the sound of geese going south fills the sky.
There is a wordless yearning or a longing
for something in the air,
and it penetrates the human spirit.
It is a tender, nostalgic desire
to gather our treasures and hold them close
because the ache tells us that someday
those treasures will need to be left behind.

Today: My inner "ache" draws me to the Eternal One.

Praying Our Goodbyes, p. 7

Quality Presence

Giving of ourselves to others
with quality presence
means we have a heart of love
and a desire to care for others.
It means that "being with"
is just as significant as "doing for."
It means being willing to have nothing to show
for our day's work
except faithfully standing by the cross of another,
or giving love in a celebrative moment,
or attentive, perceptive listening with our heart.
This kind of presence creates peace, energy,
and acceptance in the heart of another.
Quality moments
mean forgetting about clocks and calendars.

Today: I create a quality presence with my love.

Fresh Bread, p. 15

September 25

Prayer as a Form of Kindness

As Mom's years dwindled, one way her generosity
continued to grow was through her prayer life.
Mom liked to "do" little kindnesses for others.
When her health waned, praying for people
gave her a way to continue to be kind.
Her spiritual practice taught me
that when elderly people become less physically active
and unable to accomplish "good deeds,"
they continue to contribute significantly
to the well-being of others through the gift of prayer.
How I long for more senior persons
to realize the power of their prayerful presence.

Today: Through my prayer I extend kindness to others.

Fly While You Still Have Wings, p. 93

SEPTEMBER 26

A Little Space

Source of Nurturance,
I have enough space in which to grow
if I will let myself believe it.
Each moment you offer me your deep embrace.
I need only to awaken and deepen my awareness.
You can fit into the tiniest space of my life.
No place is too small for growth.
You slip into my passages of thought.
You glide through my relationships.
You flow between the creases of my work.
You pass among my many emotions.
You sail into my night dreams.
You squeeze into my busyness.
You nestle in my solitude.
Every part of my life has space enough for you.

Today: Each part of my day has room for the Holy One.

Prayers to Sophia, p. 10

Belonging to God

When I can reap the benefits, it's easy to belong to God.
When everything is going my way
and I have my life under control,
I like belonging to God.
But when I am in conflict with another person
or want to focus all my attention on myself
instead of sharing my gifts with others,
then belonging to God becomes much more difficult.
If I didn't belong to God, I could just follow my own will,
living as if I did not need to care for anyone else
or pay attention to what God might want of me.
Belonging to God requires that I accept not only
the guidance, comfort, understanding, and love that
    God offers,
but also the values and behaviors that go along
with being a person who is "of God."

Today: I show by my life that I belong to God.

Inviting God In, p. 123

SEPTEMBER 28

Being Changed

Prayer is not only about entering
into a relationship with God,
it is also about being changed.
Healthy prayer strengthens our bond
with the Creator and it also transforms us.
Each encounter with God provides
the opportunity for us to grow spiritually.
Prayer makes a difference in our life
because it nudges and persuades us
to develop Christlike qualities
in our attitude and actions.
Through prayer we become more loving,
compassionate, and justice-oriented human beings.
When this happens, we are altered in a positive way
and the world we touch is also changed for the better.

Today: I choose to become more Christlike.

Prayer, p. 20

Companions of Jesus

Throughout my life, I've been influenced
by people who are "companions of Jesus."
They are not out of the ordinary,
yet their presence touches my heart
and inspires me to want to be like them.

These persons have taught me
that to be a companion of Jesus
does not take extraordinary talent and skill.
It only needs someone who tries to embody
the kind of love that was a part
of all Jesus said and did.

Today: I focus on embodying a quality of Jesus.

God's Enduring Presence, p. 58

September 30

Follow Me

a walk in morning stillness
late September mist-in-air,
the pond so calm with quiet
that every golden-leafed tree
looks deeply back at me.

I think the passage about Abraham.
I pray the passage about Abraham.
the quiet, the pond, possess me.
the reality of following God
seeps through every silent moment.

the questions in my life this day
are walking away with treasured answers:
come, follow me. follow me. follow me.
strong wings will bear the journey,
faithful hearts will hear the music.
come, follow me. follow me. follow me.

Today: I respond to the music of "follow me."

Fresh Bread, p. 124

When My Time Comes

One heart-shaped pink pod
falls from the branch,
returning to the soil
from whence it came.

Even the most beautiful
must fall, fade, return;
all fruit succumbs,
all flowers yield.

When my time comes
to drop from the stem
and return to the Source,
may my tumbling
toward the One
be a dance of surrender.

Today: I enter October with a peaceful spirit.

Rest Your Dreams on a Little Twig, p. 57

October 2

Autumn

the season of vulnerability
when the great arms of oak
stretch their summer leaves
to the wild October winds.

all that has been life and green
is stripped from strong trees,
and the tall, wide branches
seem to be deathly wounded.

this is the season of vulnerability
when the trees open wide to wounding,
when all their summer security
is given away to another season.

Today: I learn from trees how to accept endings.

Fresh Bread, p. 128

October 3

Bearing Heavy Burdens

O Divine Comforter,
I come to you with an over-full life,
one that leaves me little time to grieve.
Please help me to bear my heavy burdens
and do what I can to tend my sorrow.
I will rest my weariness upon your heart
and trust that my grief will wait for me
until I am able to be attentive to it.
All I can do right now is lean on your love.
May your strength sustain me in my loss.

Today: I draw encouragement from the Divine Comforter.

Now That You've Gone Home, p. 134

October 4

In Time

Love pours out,
but the broken cup
cannot receive

Love waits to strengthen
Love waits to nourish
Love waits to be received
Love waits to heal

in time
the cup will be mended
in time
the cup will be raised
in time
the cup will receive again

Today: Healing Love stirs in my life.

The Cup of Life, p. 76

October 5

At a Threshold

There is a time to open and a time to close the door.
If we are going to fly freely
and step deeply into our soul,
to live with greater consciousness,
certain doors have to be closed.
When we stand on the threshold,
we will be there forever unless we make a decision
to go forward or to turn around and go back.
With either decision, we leave something behind.
Sometimes closing a door
is exactly the choice to make
because it frees us
to enter a fresh dimension of growth.
At other times, closing the door is the worst choice
because the closure blocks our growth
and keeps us trapped.

Today: I see what I need to leave behind.

Open the Door, p. 118

October 6

Death That Helps Us Live

Guardian of Death,
Why is it necessary for you to guard death?
What could possibly damage or harm it?
Ah, but this is not about physical endings.
This death is of the sort that helps us live:
Unwanted closures that widen our mind,
Unsought changes that expand our heart.
These deaths rob us of our grasped treasures
And free us to move beyond our limited selves.
You guard these times of loss and letting go,
Knowing we need them if we are to grow.

Today: I accept what will assist my spiritual growth.

Fragments of Your Ancient Name, October 25

October 7

Goodbye to Summer

Impermanence, transformation,
seasonal changes, goodbyes.
Call it by whatever name,
it's bound to leave a crusty mark
on my reluctant spirit.

The time has come to end
my light-filled summertime
when I floated on emerald wings.
Now I stand here by the patio door
looking out at naked trees.

I take a deep breath, give a sigh
of resignation, gather my precious
remembrance of those succulent months
while my memory takes one last, grateful look
at summer's dewy dawns.

Today: Memories of summer impart gratitude in me.

My Soul Feels Lean, p. 12

Investing Our Love

Do we ever get used to saying goodbye?
Or should we? I think not.
Saying goodbye helps us to experience
the depths of our human condition.
It leads us to a much deeper understanding
of what it means to live in its mystery
and its wholeness.

We ought not to be afraid of the partings
that life asks of us.
Nor ought we to hold back
in giving ourselves fully to love,
to the wonderful growth opportunities
of investing ourselves in people and events.

Today: I reinvest my life in loving well.

Praying Our Goodbyes, p. 2

Crossing Over

Companion and Guide,
you are my transition coach.
You say to me:
"Cross over the bridge.
Go ahead, come on over.
It's sturdy enough.

Don't look down, though,
or you might get terrified
and never walk across.

Don't look back too long
or you will lose courage
and want to stay
right where you are.

Hang on. Keep going."

Today: I pray for courage to cross my bridges.

Out of the Ordinary, p. 202

October 10

Falling Leaves

O falling leaves of autumn,
what mysteries of death
you proclaim
to my unwilling self

what eternal truths
you disturb
in the webbings
of my protected heart

what wildness
you evoke
in the gusty dance
of emptying winds

what mellow tenderness
you bravely breathe
in your required surrender

Today: I listen to what autumn proclaims.

The Circle of Life, p. 170

October 11

Befriending My Aging

Companion of Life, Guardian of Death,
more and more I resemble an old gnarled tree,
wrinkled bark, gray boughs, thinning leaves.
The ground around my roots is weakening.
My limbs bend and no longer stretch very far.

Grant me the ability to not be afraid,
even in the face of significant physical change.
Be a source of deepening hope
during my internal and external adjustment.
Keep me trusting in the deepest part of myself
where love and vitality are stored.

Today: I turn toward my inner store of love and vitality.

Prayers to Sophia, p. 18

The Secret of Serenity

with a constant chorus of cicadas
the leaves tumble down,
from long, thin silver poplars
they twirl to the ground,
dancing the autumn death-dance
beneath the great blue sky.

this gigantic death scene of leaves
does not smell of sorrow and sadness;
rather, the earth is colored with joy
and the leaves make music in the wind.

I have not yet discovered the secret
of the serenity of sailing leaves;
every autumn I walk among them
with a longing that stretches forever,
wanting to face that death-dance
and the truth of my own mortality.

Today: The secret of serenity influences my day.

May I Have This Dance?, pp. 152-153

October 13

Autumn's Reminder

Some people tell me
they do not like autumn
because it reminds them too much
of the inevitability of death.
The leaves falling from the trees
onto the barren, brown earth
makes them feel sad and lonely.
The leaves are subtle reminders
that we are asked to let go
of many things throughout our life.
Every time we must surrender something,
we connect with our death,
with the ultimate moment of letting go.
Autumn is an opportunity
to reflect on and claim this reality.

Today: I look directly at my death as a reality.

May I Have This Dance?, p. 154

Something Unnamed

Something unnamed
is being called forth
in the depths

something unnamed
keeps calling
beckoning
rooting
growing

something unnamed
asks for surrender
      vulnerability
      given-over-ness
      abandonment
      powerlessness

Today: I stay open to what is unnamed.

Fresh Bread, p. 134

October 15

A Wholehearted Return

What does it mean to "return"?
Re-turning indicates that I have been there,
that I am making a shift, turning around
and heading there again. I cannot re-turn
to a place where I have not already been.

I find this thought very comforting
because I know that if I go
to the very depths of my being,
I belong totally to God.
Some places of my heart have strayed
and lost their way,
but I know they can return to God.

Today: I re-turn a part of myself that has been lost.

Inviting God In, p. 71

OCTOBER 16

Inner Freedom

She's ending her job,
walking away from years of work,
not even sure why
except that a strong voice inside
keeps urging her to do so.

It's the voice of freedom calling.
Now that she has finally heeded it,
she's letting herself get manacled
in the chains of self-doubt and fear.

Some people are always putting
themselves behind bars.

Today: I choose to let myself be unmanacled.

My Soul Feels Lean, p. 16

OCTOBER 17

Celebrate Life's Simple Joys

We need to celebrate life's moments
as they come,
enjoy with reverence the beauty
of each day in the universe,
live more simply and freely
because we know that each moment
is part of an eternal process of becoming.
Who we are on the other side of life
depends on how fully
we have lived on this side.

All of our lives we are called to live fully
so that we will be ready to journey
to the other side.

Today: I celebrate life's simple joys.

May I Have This Dance?, p. 161

OCTOBER 18

Time Eases Inner Ache

The suffering and sensation of hurting
deep within our personal system
gradually diminishes with time.
At the moment we are experiencing
the anguish of goodbye, however,
it seems as though it will never go away.
We feel like the flowers crushed
and overwhelmed by the inner storm.
These painful feelings come in varying degrees
with many forms of goodbye that are a part of life.
They also come when making deliberate choices.
We say farewell to other options
when we accept the decisions we have made.
Suffering is especially sharp
when the choices are between options
that both look beneficial.

Today: I pray for patience and insight.

Praying Our Goodbyes, p. 17

October 19

Pockets of Gold

Bestower of Fruitfulness,
little pockets of gold
sing among the green,
humming the melody
of autumn's arrival.
The calendar speaks
of no such thing,
but trees rarely lie.

Summer's vibrant swelling
of sweet fruitfulness
still entices me.
Cool mornings and ripe afternoons
are too delicious for me
to simply say "goodbye."

I turn to my heart,
where you dwell in harmony.

Today: I enjoy the harmony within me.

Prayers to Sophia, p. 42

OCTOBER 20

My Journey's End

No one knows the precise instant
When death steals their last breath,
When the heart that beats steadily
Ceases its rhythmic functioning.
Whenever this moment arrives,
You will be ready to welcome us,
Your faithful love sweeping us away
Into another sphere of existence.
Your radiance intertwined with ours,
Assuring us there is no need to fear.

Today: I live my life in the Holy One's steadfast love.

Fragments of Your Ancient Name, October 20

Blessing

May your circle of understanding
and caring persons be many,
and may you allow them
to support and sustain you in sadness.

May you rest your heartache
in the compassionate arms of God each day
and find comfort from this Enduring Love.

May you trust the hidden part of you
where your resilience resides
and remember often the inner strength
your spirit contains.

Today: I am grateful for persons who support me.

Now That You've Gone Home, p. 177

You're Almost There

I was on a trail I had not traveled before.
It was not a particularly difficult path,
but I was not used to the altitude
and my midlife body was doing a lot
of huffing and puffing.
I had no idea of how much farther
I had to walk, but I was getting weary and worn out.
Just then, a family came bounding down the path.
In the lead was a small girl about six years old,
long blond hair swinging in the breeze.
She was as alive and alert as I was winded and half-dead.
She stopped when she reached me,
looked at me with great compassion, and exclaimed,
"It's not much further. It's really worth it.
You're almost there!"

Today: I look at what is difficult and take heart.

Dear Heart, Come Home, p. 157

OCTOBER 23

Journeying Further

As we journey inward during midlife, we may discover:
that our persona probably has some chinks and cracks
and may need some mending or adapting,
or a complete renovation;
that we can find wisdom in the wounds
we've carried from birth onward,
and that these wounds can heal;
that surprises of beauty and talent in us
wait to be discovered
and shared with the universe;
some of what we thought to be unbreakable truth,
beliefs, and values
is now shattered pottery and unmendable;
we are lovable as we are.

Today: I am lovable as I am.

Dear Heart, Come Home, p. 158

OCTOBER 24

A Surprising Closeness

The disciples who witnessed Jesus in his glory
could never be the same after that moment.
This powerful experience birthed them
into a more intimate and deeper relationship
with their Teacher than they had ever known.
The contemplative moment marked
their inner selves forever.
The same is true for us in our transfiguring times,
those when we know from a simple
yet profound experience
that God is with us in a surprising closeness
previously unimagined.

Today: I long for closeness to my Teacher.

God's Enduring Presence, p. 66

October 25

Spiritual Wombs

Threshold times cleanse false perceptions
and wean us from feeding on what no longer nurtures.
These passageways serve as spiritual wombs
where the soul grows stronger wings
in spite of doubts about whether those wings can soar
    freely.
Threshold experiences contain tremendous energy.
They hold the power to unglue and shake us deeply,
to enfold us with a seemingly empty darkness
that causes us to yearn for relief.
They can set an imprisoned spirit free,
nurse a wounded heart back to health,
and bring peace to a desolate mind.

Today: I reflect on my current threshold.

Open the Door, p. 95

Resolution

Old hurts, heartaches, memories, destructive
behaviors, and other wounds do not have to
break us apart forever.

The Serenity Prayer expresses this vital truth:
we need wisdom to know
when something is mendable and when it is irreparable.

We need courage to take the necessary steps
to move on with our lives, whether those steps
are leaving someone or something behind
or returning to the brokenness and taking action
to put the pieces back together again.

Today: I pray to have the wisdom to make good choices.

The Cup of Our Life, p. 85

OCTOBER 27

Autumn Lamp

late October, walking alone
in upstate New York,
my friend Leanna dying two days before,
much too young to make that long journey,
but who am I to say?

spacious tall maple tree, flawlessly shaped,
a sphere of gentle yellow pierced
by afternoon sun, each leaf a lantern glowing,
veneration the only response.

she and the tree, a lamp of autumn,
illuminating presence, beauty far and deep,
a soul aglow,
set ablaze by inner illumination,
readying, readying for the long journey.
the soul goes, the last leaf falls,
and I remember
the power of her shining.

Today: I too have an inner illumination.

The Cosmic Dance, p. 93

OCTOBER 28

The Uncertain Road

None of us knows for certain where the road
ahead will take us. Sometimes there are big surprises,
unexpected curves, deep holes and pitfalls,
or surprisingly beautiful vistas.
Each day we take another step on our path of life.
That's as far as we can know where the road goes.
No wonder scripture encourages us
to seek the guidance of our divine companion.
I have made it a practice for years
to pray for spiritual guidance every single morning.
Without it, I can get lost in my ego ambitions
and faulty perceptions of how to live.
Whether the road reveals a smooth or rough pathway,
with God giving the directions,
I know the journey will take me where I need to go.

Today: In union with the Holy One, I step forward.

God's Enduring Presence, p. 10

October 29

Gentle Things

Gentle things
sway in the breeze
of my soul.

They do not speak
or call to me;
they simply dance
with tenderness.

Gentle things,
when they dance
I am at peace.

When they sway
in my soul,
all things sad
are transformed.

Today: I seek gentle things that restore my spirit.

Rest Your Dreams on a Little Twig, p. 105

OCTOBER 30

Shedding Leaves

October sheds a few more leaves,
autumn shakes the last oaks free;
all around me the earth rustles,
dryness and death are in the wind.

My soul clings to the earthen sounds
and nestles in October's arms;
a lingering and a longing take over,
and I cannot get myself to go away.
I want to stay forever in the woods
because my grief has found a home.

Today: I acknowledge what needs my release.

Dear Heart, Come Home, p. 128

October 31

Thin Veil Moments

Divine Guest,
present to us
especially in our "thin veil" moments—
those brief experiences
where heaven and earth meet—
thank you for the quickening of our hearts,
the silencing of our words,
when we briefly know you are "in this place."
Thank you for those times
the thin veil between us parted
and we knew your love inseparable from our own.

Today: I treasure memories of "thin veil" moments.

Prayer Seeds, p. 42

NOVEMBER 1

Delight of All the Saints

Holy One,
Your wide heart of exquisite acceptance
Holds a special fondness for the saints.
You gather them into your assembly
Whether they are grumpy or glad.
You hold them close to your merciful love
In spite of any history of wrongdoing.
You welcome them in their conversions
And assist them in their ways of service.
We are your little saints in the making
In whom you also take great delight.

Today: I am inspired by the communion of saints.

Fragments of Your Ancient Name, October 31

Mercy and Tenderness

I pray in this way for the people in my life
who are deceased:

I remember what they looked like,
and then I picture them in the arms of God.
I see this Compassionate One carefully
and lovingly wiping away any tears
that might still be on their faces.
I notice how God offers them a great welcome.
I then entrust them into God's care
and offer a prayer of thanks for the gift
of having had these people as a part of my life.

Today: I envision God welcoming my loved ones.

Inviting God In, p. 115

Remember Our Gifted Ancestors

I have come to appreciate the power of ancestors
from several sources.
One of these is from the Native American tradition.
They value their spiritual lineage so much
that they often begin their rituals
by "calling in the ancestors."
They believe there is much inspiration
to be gained from remembering the gifted presence
of those who had deep faith.
I have also felt this power and blessing of presence
when my religious community has begun a prayer service
by naming our deceased members
who left behind such gifted legacies for us.
Their strength and goodness inspire and encourage me.

Today: I give thanks for my faith-filled ancestors.

Inviting God In, p. 24

Autumn Glory

Autumn colors,
Morning frost,
Falling leaves,
Teach us wisdom.

Hunter's moon,
Fields of grain,
Bountiful harvest,
Teach us wisdom.

Softening sunshine,
Transient beauty,
Enriching compost,
Migrating birds,
Teach us wisdom.

Today: Autumn reveals the splendor of creation.

The Circle of Life, p. 38

November 5

Generating Compassion

Gratefulness supports hope
and generates compassion.
The more aware I am
of the benefits of my life,
the more apt I am to be
peaceful and loving.
When I let go
of comparison and competition,
when I tell worry and fretting
to be on their way,
I see more clearly
what is wonder-full in and around me.
My heart responds more lovingly
when I approach suffering with peacefulness.

Today: I am aware of the benefits of my life.

Boundless Compassion, pp. 184–185

November 6

Treasured Memories

We are much more wondrous
than we could ever believe.
We are a great storehouse of treasures
waiting to be discovered.
When we were conceived, egg and sperm united,
a vast world of memories united at that time:
memories of the world's beginnings
when Sophia was there,
memories of the earth's turning and churning,
memories of our ancestors with their joys and sorrows,
memories of the deep strain of life
winning out over the death that tries to invade it.
I saw so clearly that we human beings
are treasured memories.

Today: I acknowledge the treasured memory of myself.

The Star in My Heart, p. 72

November 7

God of Our Ancestors

A long ancestral line of women and men
Proceed ahead of us on our journey,
Leaving vivid traces of their history.
They mark the path with their wisdom,
Fill the air with fragrant goodness
And smile with jubilant satisfaction.
You are at the head of this long line
With innumerable people of good will.
Your light spreads throughout all of them,
A great love flowing from them to us.

Today: I consider one virtue I embody from my ancestors.

Fragments of Your Ancient Name, November 1

NOVEMBER 8

Yielding the Bounty

Spirit of Autumn,
When I grow tired of using my gifts
to benefit others,
take me to the autumned fields
where earth freely yields the bounty
of her summer.
Let me become aware
of how she allows her lands
to be stripped clean
so her fruitfulness will be a source
of nourishment.

Today: I generously yield the bounty of my gifts.

Out of the Ordinary, p. 196

Thirsting

All night a steady rain
fell upon the autumned earth,
moistening every dried crack
of the bony summer,
rinsing what lay tattered
and soiled in the remnants
of yesterday.

Each drop resuscitated my own dryness,
each wet particle from November clouds
awakened the thirsty muse inside;
each splash of moisture softened the hard shell
containing imprisoned words, freed them
to breathe life upon the stagnant
empty pages waiting for deliverance.

Today: I thirst for what is of most benefit.

My Soul Feels Lean, p. 105

Never Give Up on Praying

Begin again and again,
and again,
deliberately, with intention,
each day

opening the heart's door,
seeking to unite
with the divine companion,
eager to abide with us.

Stop squirming.
Release clinging.
Let go of the binding chains
to self-willed ways.

Today: I am faithful to daily prayer.

Prayer, p. 63

November 11

Memories of a Pilgrim Heart

Companioning God,
may I look with a clear, inner eye
and become aware of how you have both
comforted and challenged me on my journey.
I want to celebrate your companionship
through the numerous twists and turns
that have been mine.
Speak to the pilgrim part of my heart.
Encourage me to find the many aspects
of my life that call me to gratitude and wonder.
Remind me often that I am, indeed, a pilgrim
on the way home to you.

Today: I recall how God has been with me.

Out of the Ordinary, p. 194

NOVEMBER 12

Waiting for the When

Waiting for the "when" keeps me
from appreciating what I now have.
Longing for promises and dreaming dreams
is not a harmful deed as long as
the present moment is not overlooked,
as long as gratitude rises for what is already here,
as long as I do not base my happiness
on what is still wanting.
Thankfulness for what has already been given
is the foundation for hoping for what is not yet.

Today: I put aside "when" and gratefully receive what is.

Out of the Ordinary, p. 190

NOVEMBER 13

Uncluttering the Heart

inside each of us
there awaits a wonder
full
spirit of freedom

she waits to dance
in the rooms
of our heart
that are closed
dark and cluttered

she waits to dance
in the corners
where we still
do not believe in our goodness

Today: I enliven more of my essential goodness.

The Star in My Heart, pp. 76-77

November 14

Faithful People

It is a gift to know people who are faithful,
people whose inner strength urges them
to share their love generously
even when they pay a price to do so.
Their lives tell us that faithfulness
is possible, although it is rarely easy.

Faithful people reflect God's faithfulness.

Today: I give thanks for faithful people.

May I Have This Dance?, p. 171

Butterfly

As I lay there, slowly awakening,
the image of newly hatched butterflies
came to me—how they

> hang
> there
> and wait

as the blood fills out
their fresh wings.

This morning I was the butterfly
allowing my sleepy self
to rest, to wait, to fill with life,
to ready my wings for the day.

Today: I pay attention to how I need to care for self.

My Soul Feels Lean, p. 108

November 16

Unfamiliar Doors

Each of us is a traveler of the heart.
As we traverse the road of life,
we come to unknown and unsought doors
revealing further truth about our authentic self.
These unfamiliar doors of life
hide pieces of beneficial wisdom.
They contain information for our transformation
even though we may not understand this
for quite a while.

Today: I pray to be a courageous traveler of the heart.

Open the Door, p. 44

Ground of My Being

There is no tyranny in your divine essence.
Rather, you are part of the cause and effect
Of this intrinsic world and of our very self.
You, the solid base upon which all exists,
Remain beyond our greatest comprehension.
We can only speak about and proclaim you
Through the guiding help of symbol and story.
Still, we dare to approach and believe in you,
Because somewhere deep within the soul
We know you are who you are.

Today: The Ground of My Being supports me.

Fragments of Your Ancient Name, August 3

Allured to the Sacred

On the eve of my mother's birthday,
six years after her death,
I arise in the deep of night.

On my way to the bathroom
a wide ray of moonlight
coming through the south window
stuns me with its brilliance.

I move toward its allurement
and stand with full attention
in the gaze
of the strong, full moon,

wondering why I feel blessed,
why this light coming from afar
has the touch of holiness,
why I want to gather it
around me like a sacred womb.

Today: I respond to what allures me to the Sacred.

Fly While You Still Have Wings, p. 183

Liminal Space

Liminal space is a twilight time
when it is neither day nor night.
Things cannot be seen clearly
in the dusky grayness
washing over our mind and heart.

Being in liminal space
is like swinging on a trapeze.
Once the handle is released
there is nothing to hold on to
until the handle on the other side
is caught.

Liminality requires acceptance
of the process of change
while being unsure and unclear
of how this liminal time will affect our future.

Today: I find security in the Holy One's presence.

Open the Door, pp. 98-99

The Old Closeness

The old closeness returned
last evening.
The solitude of dusk,
the beautiful gasp of sky,
the power of the full moon,
each one embraced me.

I sat in stillness,
held close in the cleavage
of evening,
resting my longing
on her gentle bosom.

Always in those moments
I am at peace,
freed from my bones,
at one with a home
far, far away,
yet eternally close.

Today: I rest in stillness.

The Cosmic Dance, p. 26

November 21

Hospitality

As we gather around the table of friendship,
we come with profound thanksgiving
for the countless times
we have been welcomed by the Holy One
dwelling in another person.
Because of open minds and hearts
we have been received with warmth and kindness.

We bring our intention to continue our efforts
to accept those with whom we have differences.
We welcome those who live among us
whom we would rather not welcome.

We pray to grow stronger and live more fully
the vital qualities of hospitality: kindness, nonjudgment,
understanding, generosity, acceptance, and good cheer.

Today: I am hospitable toward all whom I meet.

Prayer Seeds, pp. 46–47

The Fog

Quiet Mystery,
today the earth wears mufflers on her ears.
Heavy wet clouds disguise the silent land.
The city is a giant mound of bleary white
with dense fog permeating everything.
Even the sparrow's song sounds thick.
In the concealing mist of morning,
streetlights blur with masked revelation,
and walkers are lost in a veil of obscurity.

Quiet me, as fog quiets the external world,
so that I can listen more intently to you.
Draw me further into surrender.
Rest me in your comforting stillness,
and let me be content with what is unclear.

Today: I find quietness inside of me.

Prayers to Sophia, pp. 64–65

November 23

A Thanksgiving Blessing

May your basket of blessings surprise you
with its rich diversity of gifts
and opportunities for growth.
May all that nourishes and resources your life
bring you daily satisfaction and renewed hope.
May you slow your hurried pace of life
so you can be aware of, and enjoy,
what you too easily take for granted.
May you always be open, willing,
and ready to share your blessings with others.
May you never forget the Generous One
who loves you lavishly and unconditionally.

Today: I count my blessings.

Out of the Ordinary, p. 191

November 24

Gratitude for Little Moments

gratitude, yes,
for all the big things
that stand tall,
thick with abundance,
joy, fruitfulness.
I cannot help
but applaud
their presence.

but deep thankfulness
for the bite-sized
pieces of my life?
I had not thought of them,
those little snippets of time
so easily consumed
in the hurry and blur
of pretentious days.

Today: I am mindful of the bite-sized gifts.

Out of the Ordinary, p. 186

November 25

Wrapped in Darkening Days

Autumn God,
when I accept only the beautiful
and reject the tattered, torn parts of who I am,
when I treat things that are falling apart
as my enemies,
walk me among the dying leaves.
Let them tell me about their power
to re-energize the earth's soil
by their decomposition and decay.
When I refuse to wait with the mystery
of the unknown and when I struggle to control
rather than let life evolve,
wrap me in the darkening days of November.
Encourage me to enter into stillness
and silent mystery,
to wait patiently for clarity and wisdom.

Today: I learn from November's darkening days.

Out of the Ordinary, p. 196

November 26

Beyond Doom and Gloom

Luke 21:9 tells us, "When you hear of wars and
insurrections, do not be terrified."

I rarely reflect on the "end times" because
I believe that whenever the "end" does come,
it is vital that I be living my life as well as I can
right now.

I do think, however, it is good to be reminded
that our earthly life will someday come to an end.
When we pause to remember that we, too, are mortal,
and that death could happen at any time,
it puts our life into quick perspective.

Today: I live with gratitude for the life I've been given.

Inviting God In, p. 131

A Container of Divine Presence

On cold winter days, I especially like the feel
of my favorite coffee mug in my hands,
and I thoroughly enjoy the sips of liquid
that bring welcomed warmth into my body.
My coffee mug reminds me
that cups are containers
designed to hold something refreshing,
just as we are containers
meant to hold the Divine Presence.
Because God dwells within me,
I like to think of myself
as a mini Ark of the Covenant.
God goes with me wherever I go.
I carry God into each relationship and experience.
A powerful thought, that one.

Today: I am a container of divine presence.

The Cup of Our Life, p. 16

Divine Illumination

A brilliant radiance resides in us—
the Divine Illumination of our souls.
This radiance carries an immense energy
of love and wisdom.
Each of us bears this light every day of our lives,
even when the darkness looms so large
that we feel the light will be extinguished.
No wonder the hope-filled Jesus
referred to himself as "the Light,"
spoke of us having light within us,
and encouraged us to share this light with others.

Today: The light within me shines through the darkness.

Little Pieces of Light, pp. 51–52

NOVEMBER 29

Calmness for Heart and Mind

Spirit of Peace,
you know how worry and fear
can take over and hound
a person's tranquility.
Today I place my loved one,
with all his (her) worries and fears,
in your caring hands.
I place myself and my concerns
in your caring hands, as well.
Encourage us to face what troubles us.
Help us each to let go of what we fear.
Breathe your peace
through our anxious hearts,
and deepen our trust
in your abiding presence.

Today: I experience calmness of mind and heart.

May I Walk You Home?, p. 77

A Presence of Peace

Guardian of my Soul,
guide me on my way this day.
Keep me safe from harm.
Deepen my relationship with you,
your earth, and all your family.
Strengthen your love within me
that I may be a presence of your peace
in our world.

Today: I pray to be a presence of peace.

Walk in a Relaxed Manner, p. 15

December 1

The Disturber

Wake us up
To what needs doing,
And what needs undoing.
Wake us up
To what must be let go,
And what to draw closer.
Wake us up to what enlarges love
And what diminishes it.
In all parts of our life,
Disturb and wake us up!

Today: I become wider awake.

Fragments of Your Ancient Name, April 12

December 2

Little Glimmers of Hope

God of hope,
you never stop believing in us.
You are always present with us,
offering assurance that you care for us,
encouraging us to not lose hope.
Help me find little glimmers of hope
in even the worst of days.
Inspire me to find something to believe in
when it seems there is nothing left
for me to hold on to.

Today: I keep my focus on little glimmers of hope.

May I Walk You Home?, p. 65

DECEMBER 3

A Listening Heart

Listener of our Deepest Self,
the ear of your heart
is forever attentive to us.
We call and you respond.
We turn and you embrace.
We look and you gaze.
We search and you lead.
We lose and you find.
We wander and you return us home.
Grant us the grace
to be a reflection of your presence.

Today: I open the ear of my heart to the Listener.

Prayer Seeds, p. 129

DECEMBER 4

Waiting

Certain words are employed so often
during our liturgical seasons
that they can easily be ignored
due to overuse.
"Waiting" is one of these words.
What does waiting have to do
with longing for God's coming?
When we wait in tough times,
we are in a special God-moment.
We know we can't "go it alone."
The One who came into this world
is our Peace-Bringer.
As we wait, we turn to our God
and cry out for Peace to come
and enfold us.

Today: I wait for Peace to enfold me.

Inviting God In, p. 20

December 5

The Place of Growth

in the dark days
of my heart
I do not wait to walk
until light lingers
for I know not
when it shall come.

I go instead
stumbling into darkness,
searching for a road,
straining to see a way.

darkness—
it is the place
of growth,
and I am ripe for it.

Today: I remember that both light and darkness are
needed for true growth.

Dear Heart, Come Home, pp. 39–40

December 6

Word Made Flesh

You came to dwell among us long ago.

No matter how dull and lifeless
or how happy and fulfilling our lives may be,
there is always need for a deeper awareness
of your hopeful presence.
There are signs of your coming,
signs of your continued presence
everywhere in our lives.
Freshen up our vision
so we can recognize your dwelling
within and among us, as we move hurriedly
in this busy season of the year.

Today: I look for the Word Made Flesh.

Out of the Ordinary, p. 8

December 7

Welcome the One Who Comes

Advent beckons to us.
Be still.
Be alert.

Cry out to God.
Cry out to be open and receptive.
Sharpen your awareness
of the One who dwells within.

Open up.
Hollow out.
Receive.
Welcome the One who comes.

Today: I am alert to Advent's beckoning.

Fresh Bread, p. 152

DECEMBER 8

A Season of Hopeful Growth

Advent is a season of hopeful growth,
a time when we can bring to God
what is wounded in us
and ask for restoration.
It is a good time to pause and ask:
What is there within my life
that I need to bring to the feet of Jesus for healing?
Has any part of my life gone lame?
Has my enthusiasm waned?
My trust in others broken?
My energy to do good depleted?
Have I been blind to things
that need tending in my spirit?

Today: I ask for restoration.

Inviting God In, p. 22

How Can I Keep from Singing?

The presence of God is everywhere.
The more I am aware of this,
the more joy my heart contains.
The better I listen and the more closely
I look at where Love is present,
the happier I am,
the more kindness I generate,
the greater peace I experience.
It doesn't take much to sing joyfully
to God—simply a human heart
delighting in the beauty and miracles
inherent in every single day.

Today: My spirit sings joyfully.

God's Enduring Presence, p. 79

December 10

God's Ways of Being Known

Angels appear at significant moments
in people's lives. They act as messengers of God,
guiding, inviting, protecting, giving direction.
They offer both comfort and challenge.

Angels in scripture remind us
there is a spiritual realm in our lives
where God is always desiring
to be known and heard.

Advent is a good time to be more aware
of this spiritual dimension,
to be open to hearing the voice of God,
to be open to receiving comfort and guidance
whether this comes in prayer
or in the hidden disguise of another person
who is an unexpected messenger of God for us.

Today: I am open and alert to God's messengers.

Inviting God In, p. 26

December 11

God Our Rock

In using a metaphor such as "rock"
when we refer to God,
we are indicating that we have someone
who is a strong support, a sturdy shelter,
and a comforting presence for us.
It also suggests that we believe in a God
who is an eternal refuge,
a constant source of strength,
one whose love is as enduring
as the ancient rocks of the universe.
The next time you see a rock or a large stone,
touch it, or sit upon it, or hold it in your hand.
Let it speak to you of the marvels of God our Rock.

Today: I remember that God gives me support.

Inviting God In, p. 29

December 12

The Gift of Hope

God of hope, come! Enter into every human heart
that cries out for a glimpse of your love,
for a sign of your welcoming presence,
for a taste of your happiness.
Be the one who calms the restless
and gentles the ache of the human journey.

God of hope, come! Enter into this Advent season
with the grace of joy and laughter.
Fill faces with smiles of delight
and voices with sounds of pleasure.
Let this gift come from deep within.
Replenish all with the joyful blessings
that only your peace can bring.

Today: I welcome joy whenever it shows up.

Out of the Ordinary, p. 6

DECEMBER 13

A Season for Exiles

Advent is a season for exiles.
It is a time of waiting,
a time of yearning for light
to dispel the darkness.

The Advent atmosphere is rooted
in the experience of exile
described in the Hebrew scriptures.
The people were far from their homeland.
The Messiah would light their way home.

Advent expresses this yearning
to return home to a secure place of peace.

Today: I long for peace to become stronger in me.

May I Have This Dance?, pp. 184–185

DECEMBER 14

Yearning

Something in me is stirring;
I think it's the part of me
that waits in lonely exile
and yearns for a homeland.

It's the hidden part of me
that wanders aimlessly,
stumbling in the dark,
crying to be found.

Today: I bring all of myself to the Holy One.

May I Have This Dance?, p. 182

DECEMBER 15

Homecomings

God of exiles, keep calling us home.
You know the yearnings of our hearts.
You also know how easily
we can lose our way.
May this Advent season be a time
of coming home to the best of who we are.
May our personal homecomings influence
all the earth.
We walk this day with hopeful hearts,
believing that your justice and compassion
will bring comfort and freedom
to all who are in exile.

Today: I pray for refugees and immigrants.

May I Have This Dance?, p. 194

DECEMBER 16

Light-Bearer

Eternal Lamp of Love,
remind me often of how much radiance comes
from the glow of one small candle flame.
When my spiritual window is heavily clouded,
and your abiding love seems far from me,
restore my belief in your vibrant presence.
When I doubt my ability to be a bearer of your light,
shine your truth and wisdom into my faltering spirit.

Thank you for the illuminated beings
who have touched my life with their goodness.
Your light shining through them
has inspired me and filled me with spiritual energy.
Assure me that I can also be a Light-bearer for others,
a clear window of your eternal starlight.

Today: I am inspired to be a Light-bearer.

Prayers to Sophia, p. 54

December 17

The Christmas Rush

I look at how Advent gets lost "in the Christmas rush."
The messages are all around me:
"Buy this and you will be happy;
buy that and you will prove your love."
Sharing presence is hard to do in a culture
that keeps promoting material things
as a sign of how much we love others.
Sharing presence is difficult in an environment
that encourages us to be as busy as possible
so that we will be rich, successful, and important—
and able to buy more things.
When we are busy, rushed, and pressed,
it is easy to miss awareness and union
with those around us and in our larger world.

Today: I give the gift of my presence with each encounter.

Out of the Ordinary, p. 2

DECEMBER 18

The Wisdom of Elizabeth

Elizabeth was a wise woman,
not only because of her age,
but because of the way she perceived life.
Her wisdom is evident in her greeting to Mary.
Elizabeth knew there was a deeper message
for her when she felt the baby kicking in her womb.

As Christmas draws near, we can forget God's nearness
as we rush around with last-minute preparations.
We need to slow down and catch Elizabeth's wisdom.
She experienced a special moment and recognized it
as an opportunity to sense God's nearness.
She knew how much strength and comfort
there was in that awareness.
That's what led her to trust so strongly
and to love so deeply.

Today: I stay alert for signs of God's nearness.

Inviting God In, p. 33

DECEMBER 19

Sensing a Vast Unity

As I stand in my own small space of the planet,
reveling in the power and beauty of the heavens,
I feel a great unity with all beings.
I know that somewhere there is a herdsman
in the Sahara Desert who is also gazing
at the stars of our common universe.
I know there is a lamb in New Zealand
romping in sunlight that also bathes my skin.
I know there is a woman in India
who is going to sleep under the same moon I am.
I know there is a cactus blooming in Mexico
under the same sky as mine.
I know that all of us are drinking in the wind
and living under the beauty of the heavens.
I know that all of this is a dance of oneness
amid the bounty of the skies, and I am grateful.

Today: I walk with a sense of oneness with all life.

The Cosmic Dance, p. 46

December 20

Pebbles of Truth

Great Mystery,
For many years in my journey of life
I have searched for a deeper meaning,
One that gives purpose and direction.
I have learned that in every experience
And in each person who comes my way,
In theologies, philosophies, psychologies,
And in every form of spirituality and prayer,
I find another pebble of truth on the path.
All lead me to discover who I am and why:
To enter into the fullness of union with you.

Today: I watch for "pebbles" to lead me into fuller union.

Fragments of Your Ancient Name, September 29

DECEMBER 21

Honoring Stillness

Silent One,
as we move within our daily tasks,
clothe us with your peace-filled stillness.
With the cloak of your all-embracing quietness,
we can be assured of remaining focused
on what you desire of us.
May our external activities be such
that they enable us to stay mindful of you.
May our spirits be quiet enough to welcome you.
Slow us down when we want to speed up.
Move us toward that quiet pool of peace inside of us
where we can be attentive to your love.
In these days before Christmas,
draw us ever nearer to you in all we are and do.
Protect us from whatever drives peace away.
Anchor us in your love.

Today: I am anchored in divine love.

Prayer Seeds, p. 6

DECEMBER 22

Keeping My Heart Open

Why do I think that just because I pray faithfully
and follow certain spiritual practices during Advent
(or any other time) that God will immediately
be revealed to me?
Why do I get discouraged when I do not feel joy
and enthusiasm as Christmas nears?

I get caught off guard by my desire to control
my spiritual process.
Usually I know very well that I can only be receptive,
that I cannot force God to act.
God will be revealed in the temple of my life
when it is God's time for revelation,
not when I demand it.

Today: I await God's revelation with confidence.

Inviting God In, p. 27

December 23

The Stars of Advent

Let the Star of Hope blaze through discouragement,
doubt, and disgruntledness.

Let the Star of Kindness radiate through
what you think, feel, and do today.

Let the Star of Remembrance glitter in thoughts
of good people and good deeds.

Let the Star of Laughter sparkle in your eyes
and in your smile.

Let the Star of Joy dance in the corners
of your heart that have forgotten to sing.

Let the Star of Patience permeate
that which you find difficult and irritating.

Today: The stars of Advent shine through me.

Out of the Ordinary, p. 13

DECEMBER 24

A Welcoming Nest

nests: round, full of warmth,
softness in the welcoming center,
a circle of earth's tiny goodness,
flown from the far corners,
patiently pieced together,
and hollowed into a home.

nests: awaiting the treasure of life,
simple, delicate dwelling places
from which song will eventually echo
and freedom give way to flight.

prepare the nest of the heart.
patch up the broken parts.
place more softness in the center.
sit and warm the home with prayer.
give the Christ a dwelling place.

Today: My heart is a welcoming nest.

Fresh Bread, p. 150

DECEMBER 25

Son of Mary

That first look into your mother's eyes,
The love you beheld looking back at you.
Were you both enthralled with each other?
Her young arms that cradled you safely
Would embrace you again at your death,
But this painful part of your life was hidden
As you rested in her complete attention.
Son of Mary, child of a pure-hearted mother,
You are with me from birth through death,
Holding me the same way your mother held you.

Today: The Son of Mary beholds me with love.

Fragments of Your Ancient Name, December 26

December 26

More Than a Memory

Christmas.
Memory of the Great Birthing,
the Holy One emerging
from the womb of Mary,

coming with a heart
wide enough
to embrace the one and the many
now
with the fullness of acceptance.

Christmas.
More than a memory.

Invitation:
embrace the one and the many
now
with the same wide love.

Today: I prayerfully embrace the one and the many.

Prayer Seeds, p. 7

December 27

A Christmas Prayer

Source of divine Light,
Emmanuel, God-with-us,
your Radiant Love
illuminated our waiting world
with the surprise
of your Bethlehem birth.
Each year since then
we celebrate this astonishing event,
rejoicing in your coming anew,
not as a newborn Babe,
but as the hidden Presence of divinity
contained within each of us.
To our great astonishment,
we have become your dwelling place.
We are now your Bethlehem.

Today: I rejoice in being a dwelling place of divinity.

Out of the Ordinary, p. 45

Make Room for God's Love

"Lift up, o gates, your lintels" (Ps 24:7).

Through metaphor, the psalmist encourages us
to make more room in our hearts
for the magnitude of God's love to enter.
God's entrance needs much openness.
It is the expansive heart
that has a large doorway of welcome,
the big heart that has an entrance
through which God's grace can easily move.

Gateway to Heaven,
your love is wide and deep.
May the doorway of my heart
always be large enough to welcome you.
Come enter in.

Today: I expand the doorway of my heart.

Inviting God In, p. 36

The Old Year

the old year runs away from me.
I hang onto her sleeve
but she shakes me loose.
where does the old year go
when the new year comes?

she slips away into memories,
falls into the crevice of wishes
and ought-to-have-dones.
she waits no longer upon promises,
turns her back on might-have-been.

the elves of the old year step in,
pack up the struggles, store the joys,
tuck them away in the bulging box,
spreading them out on the psyche's floor.

Today: I prepare interiorly for the new year.

Out of the Ordinary, p. 147

The Road of Life

Another year is coming to an end.
I can feel her tug at my calendar.
I can sense her insistent movement.
I can hear her call to cross over.

Something in me wants to hold on,
to gather all the good things close to me.
A part of me that yearns for security
keeps encouraging me to grasp it all.

Then a tiny thimble-full of light
moves its way through my insecurity;
it weaves a thread of courage,
sending sparks into the dark.
Up and up it rises through my spirit
until it meets my controlling grip.

Today: I am ready to risk the road of another year.

May I Have This Dance?, pp. 18–19

DECEMBER 31

Letting Go and Welcoming

Each new year extends an invitation
to re-enter the process of transformation,
for self and for our world.
We stand at the threshold,
looking back and looking ahead.
This valuable process involves
a deliberate letting go of the past
and an intentional welcoming
of future possibilities.
We will make choices and decisions
in the coming year that will create our reality.
We live on a wounded planet
and share life in a world of suffering humanity.
But we do not despair.
The Holy One continues to awaken us.
We have what we need to bring peace
within ourselves and our world.

Today: I let go of the past and welcome the future.

Prayer Seeds, p. 141

References

Reflections in this book are excerpted from the following:

Boundless Compassion: Creating a Way of Life. Notre Dame, IN: Sorin Books, 2018.

The Circle of Life: The Heart's Journey through the Seasons. With Macrina Wiederkehr. Notre Dame, IN: Sorin Books, 2005.

The Cosmic Dance: An Invitation to Experience Our Oneness. Maryknoll, NY: Orbis Books, 2010.

The Cup of Our Life: A Guide to Spiritual Growth. Revised edition. Notre Dame, IN: Sorin Books, 2012.

Dear Heart, Come Home: The Path of Midlife Spirituality. New York: Crossroad Publishing Company, 1996.

Fly While You Still Have Wings: And Other Lessons My Resilient Mother Taught Me. Notre Dame, IN: Sorin Books, 2015.

Fragments of Your Ancient Name: 365 Glimpses of the Divine for Daily Meditation. Notre Dame, IN: Sorin Books, 2011.

Fresh Bread: And Other Gifts of Spiritual Nourishment. Twentieth-anniversary edition. Notre Dame, IN: Ave Maria Press, 2006.

God's Enduring Presence: Strength for the Spiritual Journey. New London, CT: Twenty-Third Publications, 2008.

Inviting God In: Scriptural Reflections and Prayers throughout the Year. Notre Dame, IN: Ave Maria Press, 2001.

Little Pieces of Light: Darkness and Personal Growth. Revised and expanded edition. Mahwah, NJ: Paulist Press, 2016.

May I Have This Dance? An Invitation to Faithful Prayer throughout the Year. Revised edition. Notre Dame, IN: Ave Maria Press, 2007.

May I Walk You Home? Courage and Comfort for Caregivers of the Very Ill. With Joyce Hutchison. Tenth-anniversary edition. Notre Dame, IN: Ave Maria Press, 2009.

My Soul Feels Lean: Poems of Loss and Restoration. Notre Dame, IN: Sorin Books, 2013.

Now That You've Gone Home: Courage and Comfort for Times of Grief. With Joyce Hutchison. Notre Dame, IN: Ave Maria Press, 2009.

Open the Door: A Journey to the True Self. Notre Dame, IN: Sorin Books, 2008.

Out of the Ordinary: Prayers, Poems, and Reflections for Every Season. Tenth-anniversary edition. Notre Dame, IN: Ave Maria Press, 2011.

Prayer. Maryknoll, NY: Orbis Books, 2007.

Prayer Seeds: A Gathering of Blessings, Reflections, and Poems for Spiritual Growth. Notre Dame, IN: Sorin Books, 2017.

Prayers to Sophia: Deepening Our Relationship with Holy Wisdom. Notre Dame, IN: Sorin Books, 2010.

Praying Our Goodbyes: A Spiritual Companion through Life's Losses and Sorrows. Notre Dame, IN: Ave Maria Press, 2009.

Rest Your Dreams on a Little Twig. Notre Dame, IN: Sorin Books, 2003.

The Star in My Heart: Discovering Inner Wisdom. Twentieth-anniversary edition. Notre Dame, IN: Sorin Books, 2010.

Walk in a Relaxed Manner: Life Lessons from the Camino. Maryknoll, NY: Orbis Books, 2005.

Your Sorrow Is My Sorrow: Hope and Strength in Times of Suffering. New York: Crossroad Publishing Company, 1999.

Title Index

380

386